Geoff Lemon founded pirate commentary station *White Line Wireless*, graduated to ABC and BBC ball-by-ball around the world, and has spent the last dozen years as the principal cricket writer for *Guardian Australia*. His book *Steve Smith's Men*, on the Cape Town sandpaper scandal, won multiple awards. Outside cricket, he was the longtime editor of literary anthology *Going Down Swinging* and director of the National Young Writers Festival. He has published books of poetry and essays, and still writes on politics, literature, and music.

Adam Collins is an award-winning cricket commentator and writer, having previously worked in Australian federal politics advising a Prime Minister and a Treasurer. Forever a Melbourne sports nut but now living in London, he follows cricket and footy first, but plenty more besides. He was named the Christopher Martin-Jenkins Broadcaster of the Year, and has covered international cricket on radio and television around the world for a decade. In 2024, he co-authored Glenn Maxwell's autobiography.

Bedtime Tales for CRICKET TRAGICS

Geoff Lemon & Adam Collins

Bedtime Tales for CRICKET TRAGICS

fairfield books

First published in the United Kingdom in 2025 by Fairfield Books

fairfield books

Fairfield Books
Bedser Stand
Kia Oval
London
SE11 5SS

© Geoff Lemon and Adam Collins

All rights reserved. No part of this book may be reproduced, sold, utilised or transmitted in any form or by any electronic or mechanical means, including photocopying, recording or by any information storage and retrieval system, without prior permission in writing from the publishers

The views and opinions expressed in this book are those of the authors and do not necessarily reflect the views of the publishers

Cover design and illustrations by Karen Wallis
Illustration on page 162 via freepik
Interior design and all other illustrations by Karen Wallis
Typeset by Karen Wallis in 12/17 Garamond Premier Pro

ISBN 978-1-915237-70-5

A CIP catalogue record for this title is available from the British Library

This book is printed on paper certified
by the Forest Stewardship Council

Printed by CPI Group (UK) Ltd

CONTENTS

INTRODUCTION..1

1 DERA TO DREAM: CRICKET'S BIGGEST DEFEAT 5

2 LAURIE NASH WILL HIT YOU IN THE FACE 15

3 THE SYDNEY RIOT, BY BANJO PATERSON 25

4 THE DODGIEST AUSTRALIAN CRICKETER OF ALL 35

5 AE STODDART, PARTY LIAISON 45

6 AUSTRALIA'S OTHER LEG SPIN CHAMPION 51

7 MIRACLE AT WATTLE FLAT..........................61

8 THE GOATS: BETTY WILSON AND ENID BAKEWELL 71

9 THE BRILLIANCE OF JACK MARSH....................81

10 WHEN BOBBY PEEL (GOT) PISSED ON THE PITCH 91

11 BRADMAN'S HONEYMOON 101

12 BART KING AND THE GENTS OF PHILLY 109

13 ABSOLON, ABSOLOM 117

14 CHARLES PALMER AND THE WET PATCH 123

15 CRAWLING TO THE WICKET 131

16 THE WAIKIKI FORMULA 139

17 JOINING THE 400 CLUB 147

18 FRANK THE TANKED 155

19 FATHER MARRIOTT IS NOT A PRIEST 163

20 THE MANY NAWABS OF PATAUDI 169

21 THE MIGHTY WINDIES TOUR OF PAPUA NEW GUINEA. 179

22 THE GREATEST TEST INNINGS OF ALL? 185

ACKNOWLEDGEMENTS 193

INTRODUCTION

SOME OF THE BEST THINGS HAPPEN BY accident. Alexander Fleming might have been annoyed when his lab culture got contaminated by a fungus, but it worked out for the best. Not to say that Story Time has saved as many lives as penicillin, but we like to imagine a kinship.

We had been making *The Final Word* podcast for four years, reviewing matches and talking about the happenings in world cricket, when our Fleming moment occurred. We always wanted the show to be available to anyone, no paywalls, so we set up a page on Patreon where people could voluntarily chip in, and we would read out their names in thanks. Normal amounts arrived: $2, $5, $50. The sender could choose, so one day, Phillip Meng signed up with $2.22.

We pondered this on our recording. As cricket nuffies, it could only mean one thing: a gag about Richie Benaud. Anyone doing a Richie impersonation reaches first for the scoreline made iconic by his voice: 'It's 2 for 22'. This had to be the meaning behind the number, we mused – and correspondence confirmed that we were right.

By the next episode, Andrew Tuttle had signed up with $4.34, which we knew had to mean the 434 that Australia once made in Johannesburg before South Africa replied with one-day cricket's biggest run chase. The numbers game exploded from there. Soon, almost every new subscriber was sending in a boutique number, and we would try to guess what it meant. Patreon donations are called pledges, and like us, the people sending them were clearly cricket nerds, so we called the game Nerd Pledge.

At first our guesses were rapid fire, but soon the numbers got more obscure, and people started messaging us if we didn't guess right, so we would guess again. Rob O'Neill set the record with seven weeks straight trying to solve $5.57, for the 557 minutes that Mudassar Nazar batted for the slowest Test century. As our answers got longer, and the research more detailed, we decided it was time to spin off Nerd Pledge into its own weekend show: Story Time.

We knew that cricket had its tales, but until Story Time, we had no idea just how many. The years since have been some of the best fun anyone could have in the game, as we worked through the well known into the deepening realms of the obscure.

It's not just 150 years of Test cricket: we've gone from the first surviving scorecards in 1772, through centuries of English county cricket, Indian Ranji Trophy, Australia's Sheffield Shield, women's and men's, disability cricket, grade games and novelty matches, Hungarian T20 debutants and missing Spanish number 11s. We've gone on tangents through the reproductive cycles of aphids, the origins of measurement systems, Shane Warne's landscaping side hustle, and the heart-stopping finale of *The Nanny* season three.

Along the way, we've encountered historical characters

who are fascinating, or hilarious, or enraging, or tragic. We've learned so much about the game that has made us better writers and commentators than we would ever have been without it. Our stories have gone from 30-second guesses to 30-minute discursions, digging through birth-record archives, ancient newspapers, libraries of books, and the full collection of *Wisden*. And we've had a ball doing it.

At the time of writing, Story Time stands at well over 200 episodes and thousands of tales. Its listeners made that happen. And the thing we're surer of now than ever is that however long the show lasts, we will never run out of cricket stories. There are more being written all the time.

This is a selection of a few of our all-time favourites: some will be familiar, others we're very sure will not. We hope you have as good a time reading them as we did finding them.

1

DERA TO DREAM: CRICKET'S BIGGEST DEFEAT

3.37

Clue sent by:
Martin Blackburn & Alex Veljanovski

CRICKET IS A BRUTAL SPORT. MOMENTS OF triumph and glory seduce players into sticking with the game. But those times are remembered so clearly because they're so few. For each high, there are a hundred lows: bad shots, bad luck, long and horrible shifts in the field. Still, most of us don't have our worst day immortalised by the record-keepers.

That distinction is reserved for the swinging 60s lads of Pakistani team Dera Ismail Khan, who now and surely forever hold the gold medal for the biggest defeat in first-class cricket. That was built on a first innings when they conceded 910 runs, which to this day is the ninth-biggest team score ever, and that's probably not even the ninth most interesting thing about this match.

We found the story via the number 337, which matches a famous individual innings: Pakistan ace Hanif Mohammad made that score against the West Indies while batting for three days to secure an impossible Test draw. He too set a record that will never be broken: the longest Test innings by minutes. But when we looked into Hanif's knock, we found a couple of other 337s, and were intrigued by a bloke we'd never heard of, another Pakistani named Pervez Akhtar.

Deciding what counts as first-class cricket is a funny process. You need a four-innings match with at least three days scheduled, on a turf pitch with 11 a side. Otherwise, it's up to national boards to decide which tournaments are of a high enough quality to count. All Test matches are first class, but not all first-class matches are Tests. And in 1960s Pakistan, the designation was loose as hell.

Among other comps was a knockout called the Ayub Trophy. In early 1963, only five teams played it, but in 1964/65, the Pakistan Cricket Board decided to go the way of English football's FA Cup, throwing the first round open to all sorts. The big teams were there, but also teams from the Karachi Education Board, the Public Works Department, Peshawar University. Every game got first-class status. Throwing themselves in the mix, high on teenage enthusiasm, were the guys from Dera Ismail Khan.

DI Khan is a small city between Rawalpindi and Multan. It didn't have a team for the tournament, nor the pedigree to demand one, but it had a bunch of keen uni students and a lawyer uncle who got them registered. When the tournament came around, some players bailed for exams, so the others picked school-age replacements from street games. The oldest in the team was 20, the babysitter on a two-day trip by truck and train to Lahore.

Let's take ourselves back to the scene. No money, little sleep, no preparation, and they come up against Pakistan Railways, a proper cricket team from the regular first-class comp. The left-arm opening bowler, named Inayatullah, is 15 years old. His partner, Anwar Khan, takes a return catch with the score on 44. And that is as good as it's going to get for Dera Ismail Khan.

There is only one other wicket that day, when the second opener chips a catch on 124. But that brings Pervez Akhtkar to the crease, and the next partnership moves implacably. The score at stumps is 2 for 415. The kids know they've been pumped, and figure the declaration will come early the next day. They hold batting practice at the hotel overnight. But captaining Railways is a chap named Bashir Haider, and he may be one of the most ruthless cricketers who has ever walked the turf.

No declaration. First-innings points mean a win. Railways don't need to be charitable. DI Khan get an early wicket, when Inayatullah bowls the Railways' first drop for an even 200. They will chisel out three more. But the partnerships keep coming, and Pervez keeps going. After 415 on the first day, Railways make 410 the next, ending on 6 for 825. Pervez is 301 not out. Surely that's enough? Nope. On day three, they bat on.

By this point, the bowlers must have been hallucinating. Only after the Railways' number eight has racked up the fourth century of the innings, with Pervez unbeaten on 337, does mercy come. The score is 6 for 910 declared.

Now, fair fucks to Dera Ismail Khan. They go at less than a run a ball across the journey, which is something. They hold some catches, and take four wickets on that second day. They get a couple of guys out for 20, one for 19. And they only concede 39 extras out of that 910.

But in the end, four kids from the bush have bowled 170

overs, all of it seam, with only two overs from a part-time spinner. We're guessing he didn't land them. The new-ball menace Anwar stuck at it for three wickets, never mind his 295 runs. Our colleague Jon Hotten nominates Inayatullah for the worst Cricinfo page in history: one match, 1 for 279, and a pair with the bat.

That should give an indication of what happens next. With half a day to survive and 20 wickets in hand, you'd be bullish about the draw, but Dera Ismail Khan are royally fried. A bloke has made a triple, the team has one of the highest scores ever – and this is just when things start to get interesting.

First, Dera Ismail are bowled out for 32. They last 15.3 overs. Six ducks, including the top three. Anwar Khan follows up his three wickets with 11 not out, the only score in double figures. He's already wrapped up the three votes.

So we come back to Bashir Haider, the Railways skipper who wouldn't declare. He's also the opening bowler, and he's rapid. The kids don't know how to face this. One of the opening batters nicks a ball that splits a fielder's hand open, and soon is bowled. But Bashir only takes 2 for 15. He's on the edge of the spotlight compared to left-armer Afaq Khan, who nabs 7 for 14 – the ultimate cash-in. There's no need for a third bowler. What's more, every one of Afaq's seven dismissals is bowled.

But wait, you say. Two and seven is only nine wickets. Must have been a run-out?

Not quite. Qaiser Khan, the poor bastard who had to bowl 43 overs, take 1 for 175, then walk in to bat with the score at three down for a single run, has understandably got the shits with the game of cricket at this point. He's facing Bashir, the speed merchant, and he doesn't like the velocity. He's getting stroppy about being peppered. So after he blocks a yorker and the ball stops dead in front of him, he boots it off the pitch.

We like to imagine him stepping in and heaving the shoe, like Steven Gerrard curling one from outside the box. It was probably far more innocuous, but that's not as funny. So, we have Railways and ruthlessness. At this moment, still leading by more than 900, having conceded fewer than 10, against a team of broken children, the Railways captain appeals for obstructing the fucking field.

Qaiser Khan, out for 3. Tell your story walking. The team is four down with 9 on the board. In the second innings, he'll be stumped for a duck. Hope he was halfway down.

The second innings arrives swiftly. There's not much debate about enforcing the follow-on when you're 878 ahead on the last day. Railways ask the Dera Ismail Khan opening bats to pad up again. And with Afaq Khan not even eight overs into his work, with seven wickets to his name, the skipper says, 'You know what, buddy? You have yourself a breather.'

Not just that, but in a Louvre-worthy piece of disdain, Bashir decides that the Dera Ismail Khan boys would be a waste of a new ball. He throws the old ball, with less than 16 overs of wear, to his spinners instead.

One of four unrelated Khans in this game, Ahad Khan opens up bowling leg breaks. He doesn't take seven wickets. That would be silly. He takes nine. For seven runs. Dera Ismail

Khan can't match their first effort of 32. They're done for 27 second time around, with another five ducks. One of the openers gets all the way up to 10 before being run out. Of the nine wickets, aside from the stumping: six bowled, one lbw, one return catch. No need for fielders, thanks.

In a game of records, Ahad Khan's haul of 9 for 7 remains the second-best return for nine wickets in all first-class cricket. The only one better was Gideon Elliott's 9 for 2 for Victoria, sending down some round-arm weirdness on a patch of mud and dandelions against a very weak Tasmanian side back in 1858.

At the Railways Moghalpura Institute Ground in Lahore, two Khans have taken 16 for 21 between them in a couple of hours. Eleven ducks, 28 overs, and a final margin of an innings and 851 runs. The second-biggest loss is not within shouting distance.

The youngsters from Dera Ismail Khan had stuck at it with the ball, but being outclassed with the bat makes for a far quicker resolution. They turn their thoughts to their long journey ahead, hoping that nobody from home will hear much detail.

The funny part is that Railways weren't even that good themselves. Going on to the next round, they lost on first-innings points to the Lahore Education Board, which must have stung, especially when the substitute teachers only made 159. Our mate Pervez made 9 and a duck. That was the trend for him, too. He played for over a decade but only finished with 18 first-class innings and 600 career runs.

So that's 337 in one hit, and 263 in the other 17. It was his only hundred. His next best was 81, then 35. Even an unbeaten triple in a small sample size could only lift his average to 42.85, and without that innings it was 20.2. See also Afaq Khan, the seamer with the 7 for 14, who took almost half his career wickets in that innings. The leg spinner Ahad Khan at least had a chunkier career.

Not so for the students of Dera Ismail Khan, smiling understatedly, the front row neatly cross-legged, in the black-and-white photograph taken before they set off, intended to be a memory of a game that they later most likely preferred to forget. It was a remarkable synchrony: 11 kids on first-class debut, and 11 who never played a first-class match again. On several counts, you can understand why.

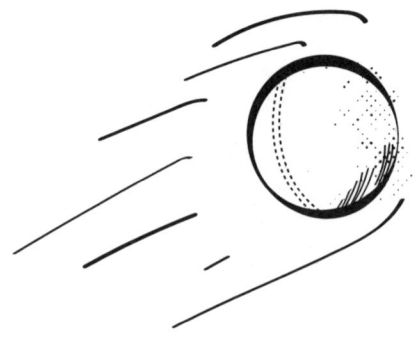

2

LAURIE NASH WILL HIT YOU IN THE FACE

4.18

Clue sent by:
Jamo

Playing two Tests with best figures of 4 for 18 doesn't yell 'legend'. But our clue from Jamo mentioned this player being a Swans tragic, same as Jamo's grandfather. The Swans Aussie rules team plays in Sydney now, but for over a century were South Melbourne, and once we made that connection, there was little doubt that this clue led to Laurie Nash. And let us tell you, Laurie Nash was certainly a legend, in terms of two sports, one world war, and an entertainingly high level of self-belief. More than any Australian cricketer, Laurie spoke his mind.

Laurie was a good Melbourne lad, born in Fitzroy in 1910, when all the guys had much the same moustaches as they do now. He was strong, stocky, and a bull at a gate. Being short wasn't going to stop him being a fast bowler. He belted in and belted the ball down, often halfway down the wicket. He was playing first-grade cricket for Fitzroy by 17 and was being looked at for Victoria until the family suddenly moved to Tasmania.

Laurie liked a scrap, on the field or off it, and his dad was similar. Bob Nash had been a champion footballer who captained Collingwood and Footscray, played state matches for Victoria, got in trouble at the tribunal for belting opponents and arguing with umpires, and at 74 years old died at a Collingwood game. That's commitment. After playing footy Bob became a copper, and was naturally of the temperament to join a police strike. Sacked, he upped sticks to Tassie with the family to run a pub. By 19, Laurie was playing first-class cricket for the state and senior footy in the northern Tasmanian league.

Laurie's combativeness was apparent. He lipped off deluxe. He was fiery, stubborn, blunt, and put people offside. He cut the sleeves off his cricket shirts because they got in the way. He wasn't known for batting, but twice in his first three games Tasmania had to follow on against Victoria, and Laurie responded by coming in down the order and smashing the team's highest score, 48 and 55 respectively. Against the Vics again in 1931, he got so pissed off that he started deliberately throwing, getting pinged by the umpire in the process. He went on to take five wickets, having already smashed his only first-class hundred as a pinch-hitting opener. Later that year he got his first win over the Big V, dominating with 84 in a run chase.

Off the field, he was just as much a stubborn bastard. His family was Catholic, but he married Irene, a Protestant, in an era when that was not the done thing. They had the wedding in Irene's church, and for the rest of her life, the Catholic Church badgered Laurie to have another ceremony at one of theirs, saying that his marriage didn't count. If we can paraphrase, he replied with something like, 'Bugger off. I'm

Laurie Nash. I love my wife, and I don't give a shit.'

In January 1932, with the South Africans touring Australia, Laurie played them twice for Tassie. After a modest draw in his home town of Launceston, he headed to Hobart and unleashed. He had Bruce Mitchell caught behind, then clean bowled Jim Christy. On a hat-trick, against the touring side in the middle of a Test series, what do you do? Bowl off stump? Knock him over, draw a nick? Not Laurie. He bowled a bouncer and broke Eric Dalton's jaw. Fuck hat-tricks.

Laurie got 7 for 50 that day, and roughing up the tourists did get him in for the fifth Test. He was 21 years old. He started with a spell of three wickets for four runs, sparking the slide that saw South Africa bowled out for 36 and 45: the fifth and 16th lowest Test totals in the one match. In the first innings, Laurie also took out the captain to finish with the aforementioned 4 for 18, and in the second innings he clean bowled Christy first ball, just as he had in Hobart.

So, 5 for 22 in your first match should get you a run at the top level, right? The problem was that Australia's next assignment was the following summer, the 1932/33 Ashes. You may have heard about that series. Laurie's wildness of character went against him with selectors who were worried about what aristocrats at Marylebone Cricket Club would think. And once the series began, it soon became what would be known as Bodyline.

With tempers at breaking point, riots brewing, and relations between the countries at an all-time low, nobody was brave enough to pick a tinderbox player like Laurie Nash.

On the other hand, a fast, angry, intimidating fast bowler just might have been an asset for Australia in a series when Harold Larwood was trying to hit everyone in the head. Laurie certainly thought so. His quotes all get paraphrased in different directions, but he said something like this: 'If they'd picked me, Bodyline would have been done in two overs.'

Confident in his ability and aggrieved that it wasn't being used, Laurie was jack of cricket, so he moved back to Victoria with his brother to take up an offer to play football for South Melbourne. He was already a good player, but he turned into an absolute gun. Massively undersized for the job at five-foot-nine, he nonetheless played centre half-back, not just taking on much bigger opponents but marauding down the ground to set up play like a modern backman. Later he would start swinging through centre half-forward and even into the ruck. Whatever job needed doing, Laurie would fix it.

In his first season, the Swans won the flag, and Laurie would have won the Norm Smith if it existed then, best on ground. In his second, with licence to drift, he kicked 53 goals on the way to another grand final. In his third, he got picked for Victoria to play state footy against South Australia, and on a whim was thrown in at full-forward. He kicked *18* goals that day. There was more vintage Laurie after the game: 'I would have kicked a lot more if anyone had passed to me.'

He was playing cricket for South too, dominating Melbourne firstgrade every summer, but every summer the Vics refused to pick him. Finally, during a gap in the schedule after the fourth Ashes Test in February 1937, he was asked to play for Victoria against the tourists. It was his first match for his original home state.

This Ashes series might be the best ever: England winning the first two Tests, Australia the next two, in a turnaround whose story we'll tell in a later chapter. The fifth Test was the decider, and all options were on the table. In that moment, five years since his debut, Laurie walked out against the English in this state match and beat them up. He didn't take a bag, but his four wickets for the match were all top-three batters, and more importantly, he went hard at them. He bowled fast, short, and unsociably. England didn't like it. When Bill Woodfull was captain, he didn't like it either. But now, Don Bradman was in charge, and he had some flint. He told selectors that this was the guy he wanted, and in this critical moment, they finally said yes.

The English were spooked. Gubby Allen was their captain, a bloke with a number of dubious moments in his relationship with Australia, even though he was the bowler who had refused to use bodyline tactics on his previous visit. This time, though, he tried to get Laurie barred from playing in the Test. Gubby first lobbied Don, then the Australian board, and his own lot in London, complaining that Laurie was too aggressive in bowling bouncers. It was class politics laid bare. Australia's board was faltering under the pressure, until the selectors said that if he were withdrawn, they would create a scandal by resigning en masse, forcing the story to become public. So finally, at 27 years old, Laurie got picked for his second Test.

In the end, aggressive bowling wasn't the decisive factor, given Australia batted first and piled on 604. Surprise, surprise, big Bradman hundred. But it was a timeless Test, so England too could have gone big in reply. Instead, Laurie took 4 for 70 to help pack them up for 239, meaning Bradman could enforce the follow-on. The third innings was mostly for the spinners, with Laurie adding one more victim. That made 10 wickets at 12 in his career, helping that Australian team do what no other has ever done: come back from two Tests down to win a series. In another classic paraphrase, he said, 'With the score at 2–all they knew where to come.'

And that, stunningly, was the final first-class match that Laurie Nash ever played. Soon afterwards he was invited to play his first Sheffield Shield match for Victoria. But we've already established that he loved his wife, so when Irene fell sick he pulled out of the trip. Soon afterwards, he rolled up in first grade and took all 10 wickets in an innings against Prahran. They're still the best first-grade figures in Victoria. Even then, his state never made the offer again.

Nor did his country, though Bradman wanted him to tour England in 1938. Without the anxiety of 2–2, the stuffed shirts overruled Don. Their conservatism won the day, instead of backing their own. The superstar Keith Miller, a teammate at South Melbourne, called it 'the greatest waste of talent in Australian cricket history', and he has a point.

Laurie kicked hundreds more goals after switching from the Victorian Football League to the rival Victorian Football Association, and when asked who was the best footballer he'd ever seen, he said, 'I see him every morning when I look in the mirror.' After Japan declared war in 1941, he joined up and fought in New Guinea, and in true Laurie style, refused all preferential treatment and promotions. He even knocked back his campaign medals, saying he had only wanted to do his bit.

Footy leagues continued through the war, but by the time Laurie got home he was 35, too heavy, with crocked knees. Still, in 1945 he signed up for one last season with South Melbourne, temporarily at the Junction Oval in St Kilda, with their home ground overtaken by the army. Despite spending each Sunday in hospital getting fluid drained from his joints, Laurie led the goalkicking and led the Swans to the top of the ladder, then into a grand final. He didn't finish the fairytale by going out with a premiership, but he did complete his career in Laurie Nash style, with the last punch of a grand final written up as 'The Bloodbath'. After Carlton captain Bob Chitty had decked two Swans players, Laurie wanted payback. 'I was after him, and I got him. And even if I say so myself, it was a perfect left hook. It laid Chitty out cold.' That may not make Laurie the role model of choice for a young athlete, but he was the living embodiment of some old advice: be yourself; everybody else is taken.

3

THE SYDNEY RIOT, BY BANJO PATERSON

6.48

Clue sent by:
Will Sandford

Test cricket gets described as a gentleman's game, but this is a lie. Rashes of gentility break out here and there, but it's still a game birthed by rascals, popularised by crooks, and sustained by the patronage of louts. This story is one of the finest examples, just after the third Test ever played. It was Melbourne 1879 when Fred Spofforth lived up to his nickname of 'The Demon': he rissoled England with 6 for 48 in the first innings – our number that led to this story – and 7 for 62 in the second, taking the first Test hat-trick along the way. In a timeless match, Australia won in three days.

Notionally amateurs, the tourists were there to make bank from gate receipts at as many games as possible. In true English everyman style they were led by a captain named Lord Harris. After Melbourne, they headed to Sydney to play twice against New South Wales. The state team also had Spofforth and won the first game easily, so before the second match the punters backed them off the map. The old Association Ground, which would later become the SCG, packed in 10,000 people.

Here, we turn to one of the umpires. George Coulthard had an extraordinary young life: by 25 he had filled out a bingo card that read state cricketer, Test umpire, Test cricketer, rugby sensation, boxer against world champion Jem Mace, and the foremost Aussie rules identity of the day. He took Carlton to a premiership, led the goalkicking three years running before the Coleman Medal existed, dominated for Victoria in state matches, became a footy umpire while pioneering what became the traditional white uniform, and got suspended for an entire season for brawling. In his downtime, he was a vigilante crime fighter, which got him named an honorary detective by Victoria Police, and he donated a koala to Melbourne Zoo. George was a busy guy.

At one stage, he and Carlton went to Sydney to play the Waratahs, a rugby union side, so the teams played once each under their own set of rules. Each team won its own code, but George was so good at rugby that the Waratahs briefly hired him, and he proved better than any of their own players. Later he was commissioned to come back to Sydney and spread the gospel of Aussie rules, but not long into his stay, history turned – thanks to a shark.

The first thing to note is that his mates took a fishing trip to Shark Island: the clue was in the name, George. The second is that he was wearing a tail coat. In the daytime. While fishing. The tails were supposedly so long that they dangled into the water and let the shark pull him in.

Now, if you think that media these days can't be trusted, 1800s newspapers were something else. Any lunatic with an axe to grind or a shilling to earn could get a printing press and churn out a sheet. So this is almost certainly bullshit, but according to reports, George was dragged metres underwater, fought off the shark with a spin-kick to the head, then swam back up and did a somersault into the boat to safety. That's boss. Not inclined to stick around, George went back to Melbourne, and Sydney entrenched itself as a rugby town. The shark must have been from Cronulla.

In major cricket in those days, each team would supply one umpire. As a noted sportsman in 1878, George was recommended to Lord Harris for the job when the English arrived in Melbourne. Being 22 years old at the time, he became and remains the youngest Test umpire. Satisfied with his first performance, England invited him to be their guy on tour. So when he arrived in Sydney, the locals got suspicious. One, George was a pro, not a crusty old amateur. Two, he was Victorian, and the rivalry between the colonies was intense. The New South Welshmen hated Victorians much more than they hated the English.

So when George turned down an appeal for a catch against Lord Harris in the first innings, the onlookers were unhappy. The English made 267 and bowled out New South Wales for 177, and the score was only that high because the Australian superstar of the day, Billy Murdoch, carried his bat for 82. *Wisden* called it one of the grand innings of its time. In the conditions, 90 was a big deficit, and the rules of the day let Lord Harris enforce the follow-on. The fate of the match, and the fate of a lot of bets, rested on Billy Murdoch. And this was when things got wild.

With New South Wales on 19 and Murdoch on 10, he

chanced a quick run. The return came in and wicketkeeper Alexander Webbe took the bails off. It was, all conceded, a close call. Umpire Coulthard, at square leg, pulled the trigger.

Except it was more like a detonator. All hell broke loose. In modern usage a larrikin is a fun cheerful guy, but in the newspaper language of the day, it meant a rough gambling lout. The larrikins had a lot of money on this game. So did the English players, it turned out: on commercial tours it was customary to bet on your own team. So with a pro sportsman in Coulthard involved, the larrikins smelled a fix. With Murdoch walking off, the crowd got up to the fence to abuse the English and urge him to stay. His captain, Dave Gregory, was revving them up from the stand. Murdoch left, but Gregory didn't send in a new batter. Instead he came down to meet Lord Harris at the gate.

For the game to continue, Gregory said, Coulthard must be replaced. Harris said no way. So the crowd invaded. A couple of thousand people stormed the pitch, including – get this – a teenage Banjo Paterson, just before his 15th birthday. He never wrote a poem about that. Per the *Sydney Morning Herald* report:

> a large number of 'larrikins' sitting at the bottom of the terrace, and within the boundary fence, made a rush for the centre of the ground and were quickly followed by hundreds of roughs who took possession of the wickets. The English team soon found

themselves in the centre of a surging, gesticulating, and shouting mob ...

With the mob gunning for George, Harris tried to protect his umpire and got whacked with a stick in the process. His players grabbed the stumps out of the ground to defend themselves, while all-rounder Monkey Hornby tackled the man who'd hit Harris to perform a citizen's arrest. Others from the crowd tried to tackle Hornby. You have to love this guy: his name was Monkey, he was an amateur boxer, his shirt got ripped off in the melee, and he still dragged his man to the pavilion and tied him up in the committee room. He single-handedly laid the foundations for cricket's first chapter of slash fiction.

Another player was heard denouncing the invaders as 'sons of convicts', even as some from the pavilion intervened on behalf of the English. The players escaped the field, the larrikins continued their occupation, and the captains met in the pavilion.

At this point another character got involved. Gregory continued to insist that Coulthard be replaced. Harris continued to refuse. Negotiation and diplomacy were required. It was time for the input of the other umpire, the one provided by New South Wales, who we haven't mentioned at all. Who should that be?

Edmund fucking Barton. Yes, that one. Then, he was a 30-year-old Sydney lawyer, but 22 years later, he was the first prime minister of Australia. Indeed, he is one of the reasons that the job even came into being in 1901, having led the push for the colonies to federate as one country. He helped draft the national Constitution and became a High Court justice. Was that urge to unite, to use reason and shared humanity to reach across partisan colonial lines, kindled at the cricket ground that day?

Barton told the captains that the decision had been fair and that he backed his colleague. He appealed for reason and good conduct. Ultimately, as Barton helped tempers to cool, Gregory agreed to continue. The crowd, however, did not. Initially cheering the emerging New South Wales batters, they promptly invaded the pitch again on realising that Coulthard was still umpire. After a second pause and a second clearing of the ground, a third attempt at play met the same fate. Lord Harris spent all afternoon by the gate for fear of being deemed to have forfeited, but play never resumed on that Saturday.

The punters didn't help New South Wales or their hopes of a comeback. It rained all day on Sunday, so by Monday the pitch was impossible. The home team lost 9 for 30 to lose by an innings. Nobody came, and the sting was out of the match by then, though not out of the story. Given what it meant for relations with the establishment in England, this was a scandal. Want to know what else happened that weekend but got pushed off the front page by the cricket? The Kelly Gang's raid of Jerilderie.

Yep. The most notorious bushranger in the land took the Jerilderie cops prisoner in their own cells, took their uniforms and horses to impersonate reinforcements, held the town for several days, destroyed the telegraph lines, robbed the bank of its cash and gold, burned everybody's mortgage debts, bought everyone drinks at the bar, and delivered the Jerilderie Letter, one of the most significant written documents in Australia's archives. Thanks for coming; you're bumped to page five.

Harris leaked a scathing letter to the press, and the New South Wales Cricket Association fired back. Another paper quoted an England player saying that Coulthard had bet on the match, only for that player and Coulthard to jointly sign a furious reply from their hotel. 'I have not had on the match just played a bet of a single farthing's value, and give a most unqualified denial on behalf of Mr. Emmett and myself to the assertion …'

The English refused to stay in Sydney for what would have been the fourth Test, instead heading back to Melbourne to play Victoria. Bad blood continued during Australia's visit to England in 1880, with Murdoch leading that side, until belatedly other English influences including WG Grace prevailed on Harris to make peace. A Test had been refused at Lord's but Harris captained one at The Oval. Coulthard played his only Test during the next English visit to Australia in early 1882: seemingly picked on good-bloke vibes, he batted number 11 and didn't bowl. A month later he was at the centre of another crowd invasion, this one after the footy brawl that saw him banned.

Angst over the Sydney riot began to fade – although after the birth of the Ashes, when Ivo Bligh led a team to Australia at the end of 1882, he promptly chose as umpire one George Coulthard. Once more, it didn't pan out so well for George. Sailing from Sydney for a match in Newcastle, he fell sick with tuberculosis. He lasted less than a year, dead by 27. Perhaps he already had the infection rather than catching it on board, but there's a chance that after surviving that murderous crowd, umpiring for England killed him anyway.

If you want to raise a glass to George, go to Lygon Street for a wine at Papa Gino's, next door to the house where he died. He had one parting moment of influence on Australian sport: sick as a dog during spring racing season, Coulthard told friends about a three-part fever dream involving him and two horses. He dreamed that he would die before the Victoria Derby, that Martini-Henry would win it, and that Dirk Hatteraick would win the Melbourne Cup.

George duly died 12 days before the Derby. Martini-Henry, a stallion in his first outing, won it in a course-record time. As the story spread, punters piled in on Dirk Hatteraick, a colt named after a smuggler from a Walter Scott novel, never mind that a turf writer of the day said the horse 'was as fat as a bacon hog.' But they should have doubled down on Martini-Henry, who made it two from two in his second run on the track. The bacon carrier finished near the end of the field. In one final salute to the world, George Coulthard had done a pack of mug punters out of their money one more time.

4

THE DODGIEST AUSTRALIAN CRICKETER OF ALL

2.17

Clue sent by:
Richard Casamento & Mike Edelstein

Some players, like Laurie Nash, are mad bastards on the field. Others are mad bastards off the field too. On Story Time, we have a category called Dusty Old Bastards: those from bygone eras with a small number of Tests to their names, names that we consequently barely know. Yet once we dig, they often turn out to be the most interesting. Arthur Coningham is comfortably on that podium. Not only that: despite being a one-Test wonder, he still holds a record unique in the game.

Let's start there: Connie's moment came in 1895, when he was called up at the MCG for the second Ashes Test after England won a thriller in Sydney. His debut couldn't have started any better, getting rid of Archie MacLaren, future England captain and probably the dead opposite of a Final Word fave, with the first ball of the match. Of course, that also meant it was Connie's first Test delivery. In nearly 150 years of Tests, only 25 players have taken a wicket with the first ball of their career. Only 29 have taken a wicket with the first ball of a match. To this day, Arthur Coningham remains the sole player to do both.

Things didn't kick on: he took a decent 2 for 17 first up, which is the number from our clue, but was wicketless in the second innings, England won, and he wasn't picked for Adelaide. It might have been to do with Connie, like Laurie Nash for Tasmania, getting angry and deliberately throwing the ball at England's captain, AE Stoddart.

In another link to Laurie Nash, Connie was born in South Melbourne, later Laurie's stomping ground, though Connie grew up in New South Wales and spent some years in Queensland. He played cricket for the latter two states as a left-arm seamer who was handy with the bat. He was quite a player: in Queensland grade cricket, he once made 26 runs in a team score of 26 all out, after taking 6 for 30 with the ball. But while cricket gave him a stage, it didn't pay much. Connie loved two things: attention and money.

'One of the most amusing features of the tour,' wrote a columnist in *The Referee* newspaper about a Sheffield Shield trip, 'was to see "Connie" in the billiard room putting over his tricks with a billiard ball, and doing other entertaining things, with Thespian polish.' He was a performer. A less flattering quote that we've never been able to find a source for said he had 'the audacity and cunning of an ape and the modesty of a phallic symbol'.

He trained as a chemist but couldn't make a living from it, then tried his hand at shopkeeping and bookmaking. He hustled at billiards. There are news reports of a one-on-one footrace in which Connie was the favourite, only for a group to plunge bets on his opponent just before the start.

While the opponent won, he 'was pretty much blown, while Coningham seemed to finish up tolerably fresh.' Who ended up with the winnings? Meanwhile, in other papers, he was flogging snake oil. 'I take great pleasure in recommending St. Jacobs Oil to all athletes in training. Having found great relief after a hard day's cricketing and running, I can testify to its efficacy.'

It was a portent for the smoothness of his marriage that he held his wedding in 1893, the day before heading to England for six months on a cricket tour. His wife Alice's views on the matter are not recorded. He didn't play any of the Tests, but gained some fame for starting a fire in the outfield to keep warm during a cold tour match, and for being awarded a medal after saving a boy from drowning in the Thames while on a boat trip.

All in all, we can conclude that Connie was an ideas man. It's just that some of his ideas were better conceived than others. One of them would really make him famous. By 1899 he had been in and out of bankruptcy, and he and Alice had three kids. In 1900, he sued her for divorce while also suing the Roman Catholic Church. His charge was that she had committed adultery with the Right Reverend Monsignor Denis O'Haran, private secretary to the Archbishop of Sydney.

This could not have been a bigger deal. Coningham was Anglican, O'Haran the second-most senior Catholic in the colonies. Social sectarian divides were bitter. Add that to a scandal about sexual impropriety by an ordained minister, and this was the biggest story in years. 'All Sydney has been sent up to white heat excitement over a coming divorce case, in which a well-known Australian cricketer institutes a suit and makes a prominent R.C. divine the co-respondent,' one paper reported. 'A claim of £5000 for damages is made, the clergyman has decided to fight the case out. The lady is said to be one of the handsomest and most dashing women in Sydney.'

And if the premise was juicy, the case was wild. Before the trial even started, a newspaper editor was arrested for contempt of court, and the reverend had one of Coningham's solicitors arrested on a charge of inducing a witness. His other solicitor quit during questioning in the courtroom on day one. We're not lawyers, but that kind of implies having learned that a client intends to lie. So what did Coningham do? Like so many divorce-court dads after him, he went full sovereign citizen and represented himself.

Coningham produced a signed photograph of the priest, and a badge in the shape of a harp, saying that after he found these among his wife's possessions, she had confessed to being seduced in the sacristy. Alice testified to having had an 18-month affair, resulting in her third child. O'Haran denied it all, saying he had given Alice the photo and the brooch because she kept hassling him for them, but then avoided her because he suspected that she meant trouble.

The scandal blew up even further, no longer just a story of a priest boning, but a priest boning on the regular inside St Mary's Cathedral. The courtroom was packed every day, huge crowds waited outside, transcripts were printed word for word in the papers. Catholics were furious, and

Coningham complained to the judge of being attacked. 'When the petitioner, Coningham, was leaving the Court, he was violently assaulted by a mob of persons, and it took about half a dozen policemen to rescue him. He was taken to a place of safety, pale and hatless, but the boo-hooing was continued.'

Pale and hatless. Repeat, hatless. Now, this may have been a man forcing his wife to try to extort some money out of the church, but Connie did a bang-up job at the lawyering part. He was up against the best of the best, a King's Counsel named Mr Want. The *Clarence and Richmond Examiner* summed it up:

> The chief feature of the case, next to the extraordinary spectacle of a wife appearing as chief witness for her husband in a charge involving her honour, was the extraordinary ability with which Mr Coningham examined, cross-examined and pleaded with the jury. Mr. Want's handling of witnesses was no better, his address to the jury was not nearly so strong. We have had able laymen conducting their own cases before … but on no occasion has the floor been taken by an amateur of such capabilities … Speaking for two hours and a half, he reviewed the evidence in a masterly fashion, exposing a weak point wherever there was one, and concluding with a passionate exhortation that certainly impressed the jury, while it fairly staggered the opposing counsel and the Bench. It was

frequently asserted during the case that Coningham was being prompted; but after his address to the jury, there was only one opinion – that he never could have had the opportunity of employing anyone so skilful and resourceful as himself.'

Like a true Test cricketer, in a match that Coningham probably didn't deserve to win he fought a stronger opponent to a draw. The case ended in a hung jury. That was December 1900, with a retrial set for March 1901. Coningham had the last huge court case before Federation and the first one after it. Edmund Barton was obviously too busy to mediate. Sectarian tensions continued, with fundraising and organising on both sides. 'It behoves every Protestant who wishes to see the Roman Catholic Church humiliated to assist,' said a flyer falsely attributed to a prominent lawyer, asking for donations to help Coningham hire legal counsel. If any of that money did go to him, he kept it and fought his own case again, but this time, with the Catholic postmaster-general producing new evidence of secret letters between Coningham and Alice, the jury found against him.

If it was all an act, Connie kept on playing the part until the curtain fell. 'On hearing the jury's verdict on the second issue, Mr. Coningham buried his face on his arm at the end of the barristers' table in the court, and sobbed and moaned loudly. All at once the petitioner rose, and, like a wild fury, threw himself towards Dr. O'Haran', reported the *Daily Telegraph*. 'Foaming at the mouth, Mr. Coningham cried out:

"I'll kill him – I'll kill him!" but, missing his footing, he fell at the co-respondent's feet.'

Things would have been a bit awkward in Sydney after that, so Coningham moved to New Zealand. Alice and family went with him, and you may draw your own conclusions from that. By 1903, Coningham was jailed in Wellington for fraud: selling subscriptions to Dr Muskett's *Illustrated Australian Medical Guide*, he was inventing customers and claiming commission for the sales. By 1912, Alice finally divorced him for real – ironically citing adultery. Coningham spent the last two years of his life in Gladesville Mental Hospital, back in Sydney, and died in 1939.

But though Connie missed World War II, his son didn't. Arthur Coningham Jr felt that he had to make up for his father's shortcomings, and he set about it in spades. He was 19 when World War I started and he volunteered for the New Zealand Expeditionary Force. Sent to Gallipoli, he was lucky to be invalided out early with typhoid, but he got well in England and joined the Royal Flying Corps. A staggering 176 patrols behind enemy lines, in which he was twice wounded, saw him decorated with the Distinguished Service Order and the Military Cross.

By the time of the sequel, as one of the most experienced in the caper, he became the 'architect of modern air power doctrine'. He led the Western Desert Air Force in North Africa, was knighted in 1943 after the victory at El Alamein, and led the tactical air forces at Normandy on D-Day. At 53 years old, having improbably survived two global conflicts, his luck in the air ran out while on a passenger plane on holiday. Near the Bermuda triangle in 1948, the British South American Airways aircraft *Star Tiger* vanished without a trace. Connie Jr was celebrated as a hero, and it's safe to say that he'd balanced out the father he was ashamed of. But his dad was probably a better chat at the bar, and 130 years later, that one-off Test record feat still stands alone.

5

AE STODDART, PARTY LIAISON

4.85

**Clue sent by:
James Tiernan**

OUR CLUE FOR THIS NUMBER MENTIONED A cricketer who dabbled in Aussie rules, among other oval-ball adventures. That sounded like it was in our area, even if it had to be someone more occasional in the football world than George Coulthard or Laurie Nash. Even in an age when it was common for talented amateur sportsmen to range across sports, the achievements of Andrew Ernest Stoddart make him a Final Word fave.

Our clue number represents 485, which comes from a big weekend when Stoddy was 22 years old, playing at league level for Hampstead Cricket Club in 1886. It would be fair to say that he was not one for pristine pre-match preparation. A match against the Stoics Cricket Club the next day wasn't going to stop him going out dancing with friends. When they got home around midnight, he decided that was a good time to play some poker.

Now, Stoddart turned out to be pretty handy with the cards that night, and kept the match going on until dawn. For anyone who is unexpectedly seeing the sun come up, there is a decision to be made: either you bail out right then and there, or you decide it's all too late to worry about bed. So Stoddy and friends went off to the baths before a hearty breakfast.

That was refreshment enough, apparently, so he opened the batting for Hampstead at 11.30am and tucked into the bowling. They were 1 for 150 after an hour, and 3 for 370 by lunch. A couple of other guys passed 90 but Stoddart was doing the bulk of the scoring. Beyond Test and first-class stats, we have records including all organised cricket. Club cricket, school cricket – anything with 11 players a side in some formal structure on a reasonable ground. The world record individual score in all cricket was 419. Going at the absurd rate of 78 runs an hour, Stoddart blew past it and kept going. After six hungover hours and 10 hungover minutes, he was finally out for 485 with the score on 811.

In the days when hits over the fence were only worth five, he rattled off 78 singles, 36 twos, 20 threes, 63 fours, three fives, and an eight – which means we must be looking at an all-run four plus a boundary overthrow. Very *Neighbours* areas, for those who remember Dr Karl Kennedy pulling off the improbable, and we're not talking about convincing Susan to take him back. The bowling must have been accurate, because there was only one wide in the innings. We're not saying it was good, but at least they put it on the dancefloor for him.

Now, this is already a great yarn. All-nighter, stack of winnings, then a world record. But Stoddy wasn't one to stop. When stumps were called, he went and did it all again. Needing to fill time before a date, he headed next door to the Cumberland Lawn Tennis Club and played five sets of tennis.

Then it was time for a private box at the theatre, and after that he was out on the lash again until 3am. AE Stoddart pretty much had a three-day bender, and in the middle of it managed to make the highest score in the history of cricket.

There's a reason the writer Simon Wilde called him 'The Inexhaustible Stoddart'. After those three days awake, he had three days to recover before making 209 in another Hampstead outing. Two days later, Middlesex came calling for a county match, where he would have been annoyed to fall for 98. He had to wait three whole days for his maiden first-class century, run out for 116. In nine days across all competitions, Stoddy had made 906 runs and partied his arse off.

Two years later came his England debut, on the first of four trips to Australia. He made a match-winning hundred at Adelaide in 1882 and a series-defining one in 1894. This was the very match when one Arthur Coningham took a wicket first ball, and England got done for 75 batting first. Later, when Coningham lost his rag and threw the ball, Stoddart was the target. Captaining the team, he was on his way to 173 and England to 475, almost as many as he had once made on his own. He turned the situation around and England went 2–0 up, eventually winning one of the greatest Ashes series 3-2.

That score would remain the highest by an England captain in Australia for 80 years, and Stoddy would become the first England captain to win the toss and bowl in a Test, and the first to declare a first innings closed. Like Coningham, but very much not like Coningham, he was an ideas man. And he lived his values. One of the novelty first-class fixtures that went on for decades was between the Single and Married teams, and Stoddart played in the very last of these matches in 1892. Naturally, even that late in his career, he turned out for the singles, and naturally, he scored more than anybody.

Cricket aside, he was a proper footballer. Interleaved with his cricket career were 10 rugby internationals for England, four as captain. He was such an accurate kick that he literally won matches off his own boot, making officials change the value of goals versus tries. After his cricket tour finished in March 1888, he stayed in Australia to be joined by a rugby team on what would later be recognised as the first British Lions tour. He ended up as captain after the original skipper died, and in line with our clue, those Lions also played 19 matches of Australian rules football. Having never seen that code before, they still managed to win six. It truly seems that there was nothing you could put in front of Stoddy that he wasn't willing to take on.

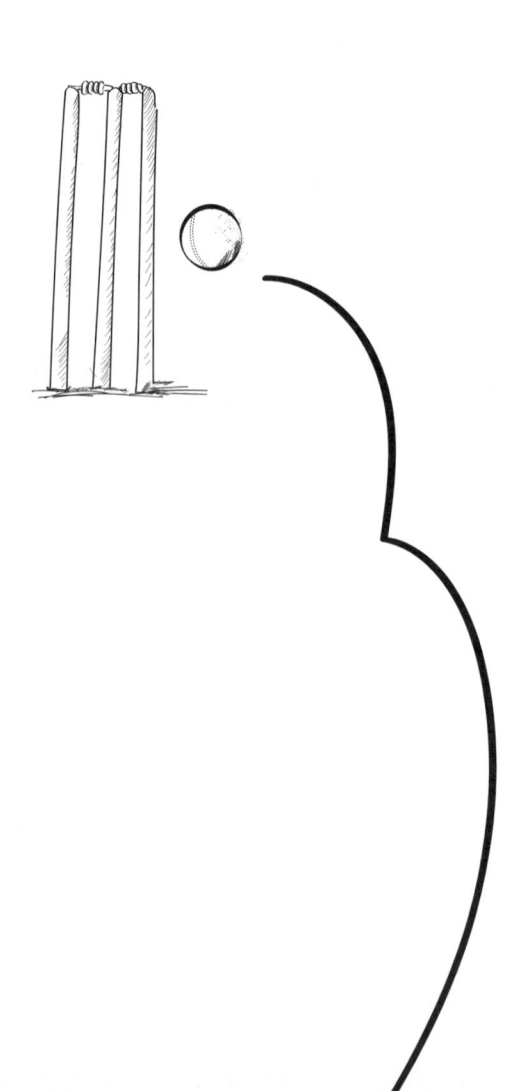

6

AUSTRALIA'S OTHER LEG SPIN CHAMPION

6.49

Clue sent by:
Helen Maynard-Casely

AUSTRALIA HAS A PROUD LINEAGE OF LEG SPIN.
You can start in recent times with Shane Warne and Stuart MacGill, back through the 1970s with Terry Jenner and Kerry O'Keeffe, the 1950s with Richie Benaud and Doug Ring, the 1930s with Bill O'Reilly and Clarrie Grimmett, and the start of the 1920s with Arthur Mailey and Warwick Armstrong. A name that is part of that lineage, but one that too many cricket lovers don't yet know, is Peggy Antonio.

Peggy was an unlikely Australian cricketer in several ways, like being tiny of stature and Chilean by ancestry. But succeeding as a woman in the 1930s was perhaps the most unlikely of all. For the most part, women's cricket was regarded with derision at the time by the men who ran the game. But some did see the light, and contrary to what you might think, there was plenty of it being played. A number of workplaces and social clubs had women's teams, which is how Peggy was recruited while working at a Collingwood shoe factory at 13 years old. Yeah, it was a tough era.

Peggy's dad was a Chilean dock worker named Francis Antonio, who had come to Melbourne and married Bell

Myra Lubke. He died when Peggy was one. This calls to mind a young father, but Francis was 55 when he died, which raises some interesting questions that we absolutely can't substantiate. We can't find a birth certificate for Bell, but they married in 1892 and had Peggy in 1917. So, Bell must have been in her 40s, possibly 50s, when Peggy was born. Peggy's four brothers and sisters were between 24 and 15 years older. A surprise late conception is entirely possible, but it was also common at the time for teenage pregnancies to be kept under wraps and the resulting babies to be passed off as belonging to the grandparents.

Growing up without siblings near her age, Peggy got into street cricket with the local boys, and by the time she hit the Raymond factory team, she was a quick study. A club cricketer named Eddie Conlon spotted her potential and offered to coach her. She started as a natural off-break bowler, but he decided to move her on to learning leggies.

By the time Peggy was 15, Collingwood councillor Laurie Marshall came out denouncing women's cricket as a 'burlesque and leg show', so the Collingwood Ladies Cricket Club challenged councillors to a match. Peggy knocked over Marshall on her way to 6 for 33. The band at the ground played him to the middle with 'See, the Conquering Hero Comes' and accompanied him back after scoring five runs with 'Show Me the Way to Go Home'. The councillors lost.

For Peggy, 1934 would be a watershed year. In February, she made her Victorian state debut against the big names of New South Wales – Mollie Dive, Margaret Peden, the Shevill sisters – and cleaned them up with 3 for 25 followed by 5 for 16. In December, history was made. For the first time, an England women's national team would play Australia in a Test series. Brisbane, Sydney, and Melbourne would host at the main venues of the day: the Exhibition Ground, the SCG, and the MCG.

First, Peggy took on the tourists for Victoria in front of 5000 people and lived up to her billing as 'the outstanding googly bowler in the Victorian association'. Having tuned up with 6 for 5 in club cricket, she top-scored against England with 43, in between taking matching bags of 5 for 24. England had to cling on for a draw.

'A tiny slip of a Victorian girl was chiefly responsible for an early fall of wickets and when the English women began a stand the crowd wanted the tiny slip of a girl to take charge', wrote *The Sun*. 'Then there was a shout, "Bring Grimmett back," and everybody understood. Peggy Antonio, a spin bowler, is making a name for herself as "Grimmett of the Girls." Soon she was just "Peggy" to the crowd.'

Grimmett was the foremost leggie of the day, hence the tiresome 'Girl Grimmett' stuff catching on in the papers. It was still better than being described as 'a short, sturdy Italian girl'. But however shallow the coverage, Peggy was drawing attention. Of course she was picked for Australia in Brisbane.

England at that stage were a far stronger side, with more experienced players. But while they knocked over Australia for 47 to all but decide the match before it began, and while Peggy was the fourth player to be given the ball, she soon had

England's star opener Betty Snowball caught by one of the many Shevills. Peggy was the first Australian woman to take a Test wicket, and that at the age of 17.

She nabbed another in the brief second innings, and two more in the second Test, as England once more dominated. But after a round of state games that she bossed for three Victorian wins, the third Test was on home soil at the MCG. Right where she had dominated England for Victoria, she started the match with 6 for 49, the number from our clue. The home team's batting still faltered, and they ended up having to hang on for a draw, but Peggy had followed up Australia's first ever wicket with Australia's first five-wicket haul.

Going back to state and local cricket, Peggy's dominance grew. Eddie kept coaching, adding the wrong 'un and putting equal faith in her batting. She had the dedication, training two nights a week plus five hours on weekends, 90 minutes batting for each 30 bowling, out in the heat no matter how harsh the summer. In December 1935, she set a new high score in Victorian club cricket with 134, then beat it in January with 142, both not out. In that club season alone she made 638 runs in 10 hits and took 60 wickets at an average of 6.1.

The press got more and more effusive. Eddie would have been chuffed by a *Daily Express* writer: 'Whoever taught her to bat knows something. The way she used her feet and cracked the ball to the off nearly took my breath. She would make plenty of runs in English county cricket.' The *Sporting Globe* newspaper put down some very ordinary verse:

> Peggy did glances and Peggy made drives,
> Peggy hit boundaries, Peggy ran fives
> They bowled fast and slow,
> But get her out? No!
> Peggy Antoni-oh,
> Oh, oh;
> Peggy Antonio.

They were even talking about her in Broken Hill. 'She has captured the popular imagination – Peggy Antonio, who at the youthful age of 18 ranks as the foremost all-round woman cricketer in Australia has won this place by courage, patience and confidence in learning to execute every phase of batting, and bowling,' ran the piece in the *Barrier Miner*. 'A remarkable feature of her bowling is the amount of spin she gets on the ball, considering her small hands, and short fingers, and also the fact that she is a woman.'

Classic 1930s backhander to end with, but let's imagine they were shooting for generosity. Soon enough, with England having toured Australia, the next order of events was a reciprocal trip planned for 1937. Peggy was a certainty for selection, but for a long while it seemed that she wouldn't be able to go. Players had to pay their own way, it required a long sea voyage, and she was no chance of producing what was then a sizeable sum of £75.

Her community in the tough working-class suburb of Port Melbourne rallied, holding fundraisers by way of dances and raffles, and the effort came to the attention of a benefactor. A director of the Victorian Stevedoring Company, James McLeod, had employed her father, and so had been interested to follow Peggy's career via the press. In memory of Francis, he offered to pay her costs. The team set sail in late March, led by Margaret Peden. They were state rivals, but Peggy adored her captain, describing her as like a psychologist on the cricket field.

England's captain, meanwhile, waited with consternation. If the 'Girl Grimmett' nickname was dull, 'The Smiling Assassin' had more zip, and Betty Archdale's description underlined where it had sprung from. 'It will be grand to meet Peggy again off the field, but I am not so anxious to meet her on. Small, dark, bright-eyed, red-cheeked and with a large grin, Peggy is an excellent all-round cricketer. Her bowling causes the most trouble to opponents, and I do not think we have any bowler as good in England.'

It was Peggy's 20th birthday when Australia played their first tour game, and she made 53 against Kent. Having first played for Australia batting at 10, she was now opening or coming in at first drop. By this point she was now recognised as the side's best batter as well as best bowler. Against Yorkshire she reached 98 while nine wickets down, and her batting partner got run out coming back for a second, so Peggy was stranded on 99. She erased that disappointment in the next game, with 103 against Lancashire.

The first Test was at Wantage Road in Northampton, and while she first failed with the bat, Peggy got Australia a solid lead with 6 for 51, almost the same figures as her previous Test at the 'G. With only 199 to defend in the fourth innings, Peggy took 3 for 40, including the final wicket. In their first outing in England, Australia had a first Test win. They held the series 1–1, Peggy topping the bowling with 19 wickets at an absurd average of 11.15. When she got home Port Melbourne hosted a welcome ball in her honour.

That home summer she captained her club, then her state. But by December 1939, as a new season was getting going, she suddenly pulled the pin. Her explanation was blunt: 'I took my equipment to the match on Saturday, but somehow I felt more fed up than usual and decided to call it a day there and then. I have had too much cricket and will be better away from it for a while.' She never came back, done with the game by the age of 22.

To be fair, that still meant she had been playing club cricket for nine years. And the decision would soon have been out of her hands, as cricket stopped for World War II, with players joining up and grounds around the country used for military camps. Peggy married in 1943 and had four kids, who by the end of her life had added 12 grandkids and four great-grandkids. She lived a long and quiet 84 years, rarely letting on that she had been a star in her day. In line with that modesty, she asked not to have a funeral.

Two more things. We said she never came back, but that's not entirely true. She played one more time, in 1949. Her beloved former national captain put together a testimonial match, and Peggy couldn't refuse Margaret. In her early 30s, after a couple of those kids and a decade out of the game, she suited up in South Melbourne, top-scored with 47, then took 2 for 52. The headline, all those years later, remained true: 'Peggy Antonio plays good cricket.' In 2025, when Alana King took five-for in that year's solitary Ashes Test, a 91-year wait came to an end. Finally, Peggy had another woman for company on the honours board at the MCG.

THIS PLAQUE
COMMEMORATES THE FIRST DEFEAT
OF AN ENGLISH XI IN VICTORIA
WATTLE FLAT MARCH 1862

CASTLEMAINE   XXII   150
ENGLAND   XI   148

UNVEILED 10-12-1962

7

MIRACLE AT WATTLE FLAT

1.50

**Clue sent by:
Luke Kneebone**

We tell a lot of Ashes stories. But Australia and England faced each other on five Test tours before the Ashes legend was created, and earlier still, before the Test era, three other teams from England visited the colonies. Let's go back to the first of these, and one of the biggest upsets of them all.

Cricket in the 1800s was mostly public entertainment offered by private operators. The modern spectator might not part with their cash to watch a few gents batting with twigs scoring one run per over on a rural shitheap, but in that era there was rarely much to do except catch the plague and talk to sheep. So teams travelled all over, partly made up of working-class professional players, partly of upper-class supposed amateurs, who were usually discreetly paid 'expenses' that greatly exceeded their teammates' wages. If crowds turned up and paid entry, tours were lucrative. If not, they lost money heavily.

Nor was touring specific to cricket. Musicians, actors, sideshows, demonstrations of strength or skill – all sorts of performers traipsed from town to town looking for their next payday. And with international maritime transport having become commonplace, big attractions from England could make big money elsewhere.

This earning potential drew the interest of two Melbourne restaurant owners, Mr Spiers and Mr Pond. It was 1862, the gold rush was ending and a depression was on the way. These two wanted to diversify. Originally, they invited novelist Charles Dickens for a speaking and reading tour. He was interested, but the plan fell through. As they cast around for alternatives, they heard a story from 1859, when cricket touring first had first gone international. An All-England team went to North America, including a chap whose name offered classic English floridity: Heathfield Harman Stephenson. The tour had made bank. Spiers and Pond were down. They offered Stevo a gig.

Our bloke had a long all-round career bowling what was recorded as 'round-arm fast'. Make of that what you will: we guess that his pace was pedestrian at best, but the ratty pitches of the day made it do all sorts. He played for nearly 20 years, a lot for Surrey with a bunch of other sides thrown in, including England representative teams against county opponents. With international cricket not yet born, that was the highest you could go: an England player without a Test cap. He did allegedly get bought a fancy hat once, by crowd donation after taking three wickets in three balls, which is one of the unproven theories about why we call it a 'hat-trick'. And he definitely umpired the first Test ever played in England.

Spiers and Pond made a good bet. When Stevo's team of Englishmen arrived, it was huge news. Melbourne's population was 125,000, and an estimated 10,000 of them came to the docks to greet the team's ship. For the opening match against a Victorian side, 15,000 showed up, and the estimate over four days was 55,000. That included the governor, the premier, and cabinet ministers. It was a carnival, with one lunch break including the country's first ascent of a hot air balloon.

Described by English player William Caffyn, the scene on morning one sounded no different to Boxing Day morning now: 'The National Anthem was played as we entered the field, amidst the silence of the vast concourse of spectators. When the band stopped playing a tremendous burst of cheering rent the air. The weather was so hot as to fetch the skin off some of our faces.'

The Vics got pumped, their second innings including 10 ducks and a nought not out. Does that mean they didn't make any runs? No, they made 91, because they had 18 players. This was the other factor. The touring team was made of hardened county players, and a money-making trip needed the promise of competitiveness. So teams like these would travel to any town, field their best 11 and let the hosts play 15, or 18, or 22. A sporting handicap let the pros show off their skills without a mismatch ending the game too quickly.

The team went all over: Ovens District, Geelong, Bathurst, Hobart, Ballarat, Bendigo, and several bigger games in Melbourne and Sydney. As the far more powerful side, they kept playing against teams with more players and kept on beating them, often by an innings. They lost twice all tour. The first took a combined team from the best of Victoria and New

South Wales, fielding 22 players to the English 11, that still barely scraped over the line. Ending at 9 for 35 in the chase, with nobody having passed single figures, the colonial team probably would have lost if chasing 30 more.

The other loss, though, was right at the other end of the scale for supposed advantage. Yes, it was still to 22 players, but they were 22 farmers and knockabouts, residents of the small Victorian town of Castlemaine, who made their fortress at the local ground named Wattle Flat.

Everyone was there. 'On the occasion of the grand match yesterday, business was almost entirely suspended in the town, and most of the surrounding districts were similarly affected,' reported the *Castlemaine Advertiser*. England got bowled out for 80, but that wasn't a bad score in that era. A feller from down the road at Fryers Creek named John Webster Amos took 7 for 13.

But as soon as England took the ball, Stevo nabbed the first wicket, and boy did it roll on. For a sequence on a scorecard, try reading this aloud.

0, 5, 0, 17, 3, 2, 0, 0, 1, 0, 0, 10, 1, 0, 1, 0, 2, 3 not out, 1, 0, 1, 0.

So that's 10 ducks and five ones, out of 22 batters, in a score of 54. George Griffith for the tourists took 13 wickets for 18 runs, and while the scorer might just have got lazy noting down catches, the card suggests that 12 of them were bowled. It must have been a brutal effort to be subjected to, and on that showing, a deficit of 26 for Castlemaine might as well have been a thousand.

But the local lads were not discouraged. Our friend Amos only added one wicket in the third innings, but his teammate John Brooker cleaned up with 6 for 6. That kept the English to a manageable 68, and Stevo was pissed. The skipper, reported the local paper, spouted off at the lunch break: 'in explanation of the bad fortune that had attended the Englishmen in that day's play, [Stephenson] said that he attributed it entirely to the bad ground'. Sure, classic – blame the facilities.

Picture the chaos of this match. Our research might be faulty, but apparently teams of 22 players didn't just have a longer batting order; they were allowed to have them all fielding at the same time. These English pros would have been trying to work the ball into the smallest gaps or hit over thickets of fielders. In the meantime, the whole third innings happened on the Saturday, so the entire town and district would have been down there cheering every wicket. The home team would have merged into the home supporters near the boundary line, an indistinguishable and claustrophobic mass of humanity surrounding them.

Even so, when normal service resumed in the fourth innings with the regulation 13 players on the pitch, the scores in the match and Castlemaine's first showing with the bat suggested that 95 was too many to chase. But by stumps on Saturday, they were still in the game at 4 for 40. In the circumstances, first drop Robert Manning making 11 was a significant score. More importantly, Charles Makinson – who would later play twice for Victoria – was 19 not out. The town sat through church on Sunday daring to hope.

On Monday, Makinson went on to 36, including the only boundary of the innings, before being bowled. The card proceeded much like the first innings: 4, 0, 3, 2, 3, 1, 1, 2, 0, 0, 1, 3. But, crucially, there were fewer ducks. Each tiny score brought the target closer. Between times they kept hustling, taking byes and leg byes, the extras total mounting past 10, past 15, up towards 20. But the wicket column was doing the same. Castlemaine had already been hurt up top by Griffith again, then saw a run of wickets through the middle for Charles Lawrence, who went on to emigrate to Australia and would later captain the Aboriginal XI tour to England of 1868.

Lawrence bagged the 14th wicket, the 15th, the 16th. Nerves jangled. A tiny partnership of 6 or 7 saw the score creep within a few runs of the target. Then another wicket for Lawrence, dismissing the player for 3, and another for Griffith, a duck.

Castlemaine had their number 20 at the crease, with two left in the sheds. Being carded at 21 or 22 would not do wonders for the confidence. Those three players collectively had scored one run in the first innings. But out there with them was the fabulously named Joseph Dolphin, ready to launch a Flipper rescue. Sure, his innings totalled 6 not out, but it was a 6 not out that would reverberate through the life of the town. With the winning strike, Dolphin carried Castlemaine past their target, not to 95 runs but to 96. Like Forrest Gump, he just kept on running.

So the boys from Castlemaine won the match at Wattle Flat, defeating England's finest by making 150 runs across two innings – and there's the number from our clue. Griffith added 9 for 28 in the second dig, another seven of them bowled, so had match figures of 22 wickets for 46, but the locals were still the ones who got to celebrate.

'It has been reserved for the Castlemaine district to achieve a victory which other much more pretentious districts failed to win,' crowed the *Mount Alexander Mail*. They were less happy about the English blaming the deck. 'It strikes us that this mode of accounting for the victory of the Castlemaine men sounds very like twaddle,' the paper continued. 'No doubt it is annoying to be defeated by a number of amateur cricketers, but … whatever might have been the demerits of the ground, it was played on by both sides.'

Ding ding ding, cricket cliché jar. A hundred years later, the people of Castlemaine were still sufficiently pleased with themselves to put up a plaque commemorating the win, which England's then-captain Colin Cowdrey agreed to unveil. He was the fifth touring skipper to visit Castlemaine, because such was the respect given to Wattle Flat following Stevo's trip that three later touring sides also played matches there, the little ground hosting some of the greatest to play the game and linking back to some of our favourite stories.

WG Grace took his team there in 1874, and his key bowler was England's first Test captain, James Lillywhite, who took 10 wickets in each innings.

Ivo Bligh's team played Castlemaine during the first Ashes tour in 1882, before George Coulthard fell sick, though we don't know if George had the pleasure of donning the white jacket and popping the finger up.

And in 1887, our man AE Stoddart walked away with 8 for 27, and we can only hope that Castlemaine then gave him a good night on the tiles.

The team continued to hold its own, with Grace's team winning narrowly and the other two matches drawn. Eventually, Wattle Flat cricket ground became a pony club and a recreation area, and there is no longer an oval where those games were played. But they say that some ghosts may be heard when you pass by the cricket ground: mostly Heathfield Harman Stephenson complaining about the pitch.

8

THE GOATS: BETTY WILSON AND ENID BAKEWELL

1.03:

Clue sent by:
George Norman

21.12:

Clue sent by:
Chris Dobbins

WE CAN SAY IT ABOUT MOST WOMEN'S cricketers, but it's especially true of Betty Wilson and Enid Bakewell: they should have played a hell of a lot more Test cricket. One was Australian, one English, they played in different eras. What they shared was the ability to use very limited opportunities to perform an incredibly rare feat.

In over 2500 men's Tests, only three have seen a player make a century and take 10 wickets in a match. Imran Khan, Ian Botham, and Shakib Al Hasan are three of the most significant all-rounders to have played the game. Meanwhile, barely 150 women's Tests have already seen it twice.

Both those players had long waits to even get a start in international cricket. Like Peggy Antonio, Betty Wilson learned the game in the tough streets and laneways of working-class Collingwood, and was playing for Victoria by her mid-teens. But being a few years younger, Betty didn't have the chance to grow tired of cricket before World War II. Turning 20 a fortnight before Japan bombed Pearl Harbour, Betty had to wait for her higher cricket honours until 1948; she was 26 when the Australians hopped over to

Wellington to play New Zealand.

Nine of that XI were on debut, given Australia's most recent Test had been Peggy's last outing way back in 1937. New Zealand hadn't played since 1935, with only one player still standing. With everyone equally inexperienced, it was Betty who showed her class, as a batting gun whose off breaks were top flight. She and Una Paisley added 163, and Betty was on track to be the first Australian woman to make a Test century. But she made a mistake on 90, was caught, and Una went on to secure that honour instead.

With a shrug, Betty went on to become the first woman from any country to take 10 wickets in a match: 4 for 37 and 6 for 28 either side of the follow-on. That meant she almost landed the 10 wickets and century double on debut, which would have been an even greater level of ridiculousness. The next closest ever on debut is JK Lever with 10 wickets and a score of 53.

The New Zealand match was also notable for a very rare instance of what we might call a platinum-level Thanks For Coming. Usually, a TFC means a player not getting a bat or a bowl, but the top tier includes no catches or run-outs. Thelma McKenzie was due in next when Australia declared on 6 for 338. The Aussies used seven bowlers, but she didn't get an over. The worst part was that Thelma was usually a wicketkeeper, but Lorna Larter got that job. So Thelma didn't bat, didn't bowl, didn't take a catch: to date, this is the only top-tier TFC in a women's Test. Some stats websites list three West Indies players from 1976, but that's from an incomplete scorecard that didn't record their batting.

If you're curious, there's a longer list of men's players who didn't bat, bowl, or effect a dismissal during a Test, but most of those involve matches that were largely washed out, players who were injured early in a match, or late-match substitutes for concussion or covid. There are 13 platinum TFCs in men's Test cricket, where players were available for a full match that had most of its overs bowled but didn't get a stat on the scorecard. All of those players at least got other opportunities. Thelma was 32 years old on debut, and that was her only Test.

Australia's next outing was nine months later, and while Thelma wasn't there in Adelaide, Betty Wilson certainly was. Another century partnership with Una Paisley started things off, reversing an early slump of 3 for 19. This time, though, Betty made up for missing her hundred in Wellington, going on to 111 out of 213. The brilliantly named Joyce Christ was the only other Australian who made double figures.

But while England batted more overs than Australia, they forgot to score, making a painful 72. Betty took 6 for 23, rattled up 22 declaration runs in her second innings, then took three more wickets in bowling them out. With women's Tests of the era only lasting three days, draws were the norm, and wins had to be chased hard. Two matches into her career, Betty had two wins, 19 wickets at 6.68, and 223 runs at 74.3 Outrageous.

Australia won that series, and Betty was vital again in England in 1951: top score with 81 in protecting a draw at Scarborough, vital runs and wickets in a very narrow win at Worcester. The series was drawn, Australia retaining the notional urn. With so little women's cricket on the agenda, the summer of 1957/58 was Australia's next assignment – and Betty's last, at age 36.

The first Test in Sydney was a washout, and the next in Melbourne lost its first day. Down at Junction Oval, where Laurie Nash ran around a decade earlier in his last season for the Swans, evidence suggests that the pitch was ruined. Australia got shot out for 38. It was the lowest score in a women's Test and would still be to this day, had Australia not turned around and reciprocated, bowling out England for 35.

Where England captain Mary Duggan had taken 7 for 6 then top-scored with 12, Betty Wilson top-scored with 12 then took 7 for 7. She took the final four wickets in five balls, including the first women's Test hat-trick. All up, the haul took her 10.3 overs, which is the clue from George at the top of the chapter.

But by the end of the day, the pitch must have dried out: four more Australian wickets had fallen, but the score was 66, and Betty was not out on 27. Her single-handed performance continued on day three, building up to an even 100 before she was bowled, Australia soon declaring at 202.

With 64 overs to push for the win, they gave it a shake. Three wickets off the top for Ruth Dow, then a burst from Betty through the middle, taking 4 for 9. Dow came back for the eighth, caught by Faith Coulthard, the first Aboriginal player to represent Australia in any national team. But with only one batter left in the sheds, the English held on.

After 10 wickets and a score of 90 in her first Test, then

a ton and nine wickets in her second, Betty Wilson finally sealed the deal in her ninth: a century and 11 wickets in the match. She was the first – man or woman – to do it, having already nearly done it twice. After another hundred plus a six-for in Adelaide, then a solid outing in Perth to finish a drawn series, she ended her career of 10 years with a batting average of 57 and a bowling average of 11.

Ten years later, Enid Bakewell would start a similar Test career in England: plenty of years, not enough matches, a batting average of nearly 60, a bowling average of 16, and the Test match double of a century plus a 10-wicket match. She also got to play one-day cricket, averaging 35 with the stick and precisely 21.12 with the ball, which is the second Nerd Pledge number from Chris that led to this double tale.

Like Betty, Enid didn't debut until well into her 20s. Playing for Nottingham's county team as a teenager, she was overlooked for England selection as a youngster in 1963 and was pregnant when the next chance came in 1966. When she finally got there in 1968, travelling to Australia and New Zealand, she already had one small child. That didn't distract her: she made 113 on debut at Adelaide Oval and topped 1000 runs and 100 wickets on tour. She played until she was six months pregnant with baby number two and soon had a third to look after while still in her early years of international cricket.

But then, Enid Bakewell wasn't very good at being told what to do. At that time, most women who got married stopped playing high-level sport and tended to stop working too. Enid thought that was nonsense, and her husband agreed.

She carried on her fitness training by running with her pram. She carried on as a PE teacher. When the school told her that letting the girls play cricket was unladylike, she set up an after-school club and recruited students to play there. When one-day cricket got going in the 1970s, she made a ton on debut in that format too, then another hundred to win the first World Cup final.

Her last Test was in 1979, against the West Indies at Edgbaston. Things started well for England: 214 declared at four down, bowl out the oppo for 188. Enid opened the batting to make 68, then took three-for. But in the second innings, with that small lead, English wickets started falling. Five ducks, three single-figure scores, a 15 and a 16. Among all that was Enid Bakewell, diminutive and fleet of foot, calmly making her way to a century. She carried her bat, making 112 not out in a score of 164.

Final Word listeners will know we're obsessed with the Bannerman, which is an innings where one player makes most of the team's runs. This is the game's most satisfying record because it was set in the very first Test innings in 1877. Charles Bannerman, having faced the first ball of the match, made 165 unbeaten in a score of 245. He contributed 67.35 per cent of the team's runs that day, and no man has bettered his Test record. But on this day in 1979, in the women's game, Enid notched up 68.29 per cent.

Nor was she done. With less than a day to clinch the win, Enid took the first five wickets with her off spin to open up the game. Then as West Indies skipper Patricia Whittaker surged towards the victory target with a score of 65, Enid came back into the fray to pick up two more, including the winning wicket. She had 7 for 61, holding off the West Indies by 24 runs. She had a century and 10 wickets in a Test, and like Betty Wilson, had done it before anyone in the men's game. To top it off, for us at least, the match ended on the 3rd of July, Bannerman's birthday.

So Enid left Test cricket on a high, but she never left cricket itself. She played at county level into her 50s, club cricket into her 70s, and she has been a decades-long fixture at Cricket Week in Colwall, both at the games and the fancy-dress parties. As late as 2022, she toured Australia again at 82 years old, with the East Anglian Veteran Ladies club. They played men's vet teams, and while arthritis meant she had to ask rival captains to let her bowl underarm, she was still batting with precise footwork and an upright blade, and was even spotted behind the stumps. One thing you can say about Enid Bakewell: she wanted it enough.

9

THE BRILLIANCE OF JACK MARSH

2.66

Clue sent by:
Richard Jones

IF YOU WANT A POINTER ON WHY LONG-AGO England captain Archie MacLaren was a colossal dickhead, Australian batsman Bill Ponsford offers a case study. Ponsford was a run-scoring beast, one who started his work a few years before Don Bradman took scoreboard gluttony to an even more consistent level. The two still share the Australian Test partnership record with 451, when Ponsford made the 266 runs reflected in our number at the top of the chapter. In Tests overall, with unlucky mishaps curtailing some performances, Ponsford finished a sliver shy of the greats, averaging 48.22. But he played a lot less than most, retiring aged 34 after only 29 Tests.

At first-class level, though, he gets about as close to Bradman as anyone, averaging 65.18 with a penchant for going large. Thirteen times he went past 200, and while 17 players have matched or bettered that tally, they all needed far more opportunities to do so. Ponsford played 162 times; several on that list played over 800. Astoundingly, this means that Ponsford made a double century for every dozen matches played. Of that group, predictably, only Bradman did it more frequently.

It didn't take Ponsford long to start, either. In 1923, after two matches and one century for Victoria, our man walked onto the MCG and spent two days on an innings of 429. Victoria topped a thousand runs, and to this day, Tasmania's defeat by an innings and 666 remains second in the record book to a team you might have heard of by the name of Dera Ismail Khan.

Unsurprisingly, 429 was also a record individual score, just so happening to pass the mark set 28 years earlier by one Archibald Campbell MacLaren. With a surfeit of grace, Archie wrote a congratulatory letter … No, no he didn't do that. Rather, his letter was to the Victorian Cricket Association, and his next letter was to *Wisden*, using his ringside view from the other side of the planet to complain that the quality of teams was too low, and thus demand that somebody, anybody, strip first-class status from the match and reinstate his record at the top of the list.

Naturally, he was ignored. A couple of years later, Ponsford buried the old goat once and for all by beating both their previous scores, this time making 437 against Queensland. It completed a feat that stood alone for nearly 80 years, and which has only been matched since by Brian Lara: they are the only two first-class players to score an innings of 400 twice. Nor was Ponsford done after the quad century, going on to top a thousand runs in three matches: 437, 202, 38, 336. He may not average 50 in Tests, but Bill Ponsford has a stand at the MCG named after him, and now you know a couple of thousand of the reasons why.

All of which is really to say, aside from Bill being a mensch, MacLaren was a colossal knob. Our Nerd Pledge number of 2.66 took our research from Bill to MacLaren, and subsequently to the worst example of MacLaren's personality. This had already taken place back in 1902, when he was captaining England on an Ashes tour, when what was at the very least a fit of cowardice saw him effectively end the career of Jack Marsh.

Marsh was fast in every sense. No relation to later Australian cricketers of the name, he came from Yulgilbar, in northern New South Wales near the Queensland border, inland from Yamba and Byron Bay. He travelled to Sydney as a young man to make a living from sprinting, and while timekeeping then was rudimentary, contemporary records twice clocked his 100 yards at under 10 seconds. Soon he realised that he could let go of a ball at the end of his run and began dominating for South Sydney Cricket Club. Just as quickly, he began to be accused of throwing.

Vanishingly few Aboriginal cricketers have played first-class cricket – small surprise given its establishment was so hostile. From the game's Australian beginnings in the 1850s until things changed modestly in the 2000s, we can name eight. The first two got a match apiece after winning fame on the 1868 Aboriginal tour to England. The next three were contemporaries Marsh and Alec Henry, then Eddie Gilbert in the 1930s. Those three were all hounded out of the game by way of bowling actions.

Marsh was rapid, cut the ball prodigiously into the stumps, and could make anyone look ordinary. Those opponents were almost exclusively white, while he had a notably dark complexion. So yeah, plenty of bowlers have been called for throwing, but it's facetious to argue that in the colonial 1890s and 1900s, race wasn't a factor. Marsh's extreme talent and extreme pace won him some support and opportunity despite prejudice, but there were also people bobbing up to get in his way.

Three potent seasons with South Sydney saw him picked for a NSW Colts trial match against the senior state team in 1900. The only umpire who had previously called him in club cricket did the same in this match, but around those no balls Marsh dismissed five Test players, including legend of the day Victor Trumper clean bowled. In a move that Muttiah Muralitharan echoed a century later, Marsh hatched a plan to prove his action clean, returning the next day with his bowling arm strapped rigid and a letter from the hospital he'd visited confirming that the splint would prevent any bending. Umpire Billy Curran quit on the spot.

That match's success saw Marsh picked for New South Wales. He racked up 24 wickets in four state games, including plenty with Test caps, but again had his action targeted by one umpire, this time the Victorian Bob Crockett, who already regarded himself as a crusader against throwing. Much of the public was surprisingly supportive of Marsh. Victorian spectators booed Crockett and called him a cheat. Test cricketer Jack Worrall noted the 'great reception from the crowd' as the bowler essayed his 'most peculiar, zig-zag run – something like the movement of a snake. His fast ball has a lot of pace in it'.

But Monty Noble wasn't on board. Somehow taking power as a one-man New South Wales selection panel, the sometime state captain spent the next season refusing to pick Marsh at all. Marsh was still monstering clubs: at one point he nabbed 8 for 32 after an opening burst of 5 for 0. With a Sydney Test approaching, almost because of his Sheffield Shield exclusion, there was growing public sentiment to pick him. *The Sportsman*, *Daily Telegraph*, *Sydney Morning Herald*, *Bulletin*, and *Evening News* all published articles and reader letters in support. He was frozen out again when New South Wales played the English, but the tourists had one date left before the Test: a rural Western District team. The Bathurst Cricket Association stepped in to pick Jack Marsh.

At this point, like any peevish nobleman, MacLaren flipped his top hat. He launched off letters to anyone he could think of, demanding the invitation be rescinded. Absurdly, he claimed that this was a principled stance against throwing, despite the fact that he'd never seen Marsh bowl. Add to the mix the fact that MacLaren had hired Crockett as his team's touring umpire earlier in the tour, only to sack him after a few games citing 'incompetency'. So MacLaren condemned the decision-making of the only first-class official ever to question Marsh's action, while citing that official's judgement as good reason to boycott the player. As the *Sydney Mail* pointed out, Marsh's action had been 'passed by all the Sydney umpires this year'.

Now, might there be a more plausible explanation, for

a captain who wasn't too worried about throwing when accusations were made against one of his Lancashire players in 1901? One, might it be that Jack Marsh was too fast and too scary, worrying England's captain that this new bowler would rip up his side in the Sydney Test if a good Bathurst outing commanded a spot? Two, might it be a simpler matter of race? To call any bluff, Marsh offered to play at Bathurst without bowling. Still MacLaren refused.

To their credit, the Bathurst Association had several meetings where they voted to support Marsh. First, delegating correspondence to an underling, MacLaren emphasised a newly amended law that both umpires could call no balls, de facto threatening to have the umpire on his payroll call Marsh for throwing regardless of which end the bowler took. After Bathurst repeatedly held firm, MacLaren eventually put them over a barrel by point-blank refusing to travel for a match that had already been advertised and ticketed. By force, he got his way.

With the power that English establishment thinking wielded in Australia, and with the risk that MacLaren might repeat the tantrum if Marsh got selected in Sydney, this episode kiboshed Marsh's chance of an international career. An Aboriginal man playing Test cricket for Australia could have come a year after the new country was federated, and almost a century before Jason Gillespie eventually did it in 1996.

Instead, Marsh only played a couple more times for New South Wales when Monty Noble wasn't picking the team. The good citizens of Bathurst tried to make up for the episode: two years later, when the next England team toured, they picked him again, and this time the English didn't sulk in the corner. Another objectionable captain, Plum Warner, did trash talk Marsh's action, so Jack rocked up, clean bowled him for bugger all, and took 5 for 55. Bathurst would've won if they had more than two days to play.

But that was that. Marsh faded away from sport into itinerancy. In his early 40s, an hour down the road from Bathurst in the town of Orange, he was kicked to death after an argument outside a pub by a pair of drunk white bookmakers. In the Australia of that era, it's some surprise that his killers, John Hewitt and Walter Stone, were called to court for 'felonious killing', but no surprise that they were let off without even having to present a defence. Those two have the ignominy of having no other place in history, but more notable names still deserve to carry their share of shade.

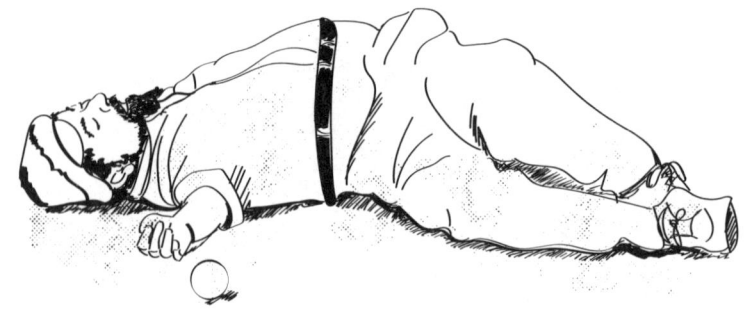

10

WHEN BOBBY PEEL (GOT) PISSED ON THE PITCH

5.18

Clue sent by:
Dominic Richards

FOR SOME REASON, MOST OF OUR FAVOURITE cricket characters are old spinners. India and the West Indies had a bunch in the 1950s, Australia a posse in the 1930s, but the best era for the species was the late 1800s. These slow merchants had stern monochrome portraits, big moustaches, and names like Johnny Briggs, Tom McKibbin, Billy Bates, Joey Palmer, Hugh Trumble. They were rarely called spinners then, just slow bowlers, and they looped down an array of strange deliveries on uncovered pitches that were all variety of soft, damp, spongy, and erratic. When it comes to Bobby Peel, his most prominent tales all involve, in one way or another, too much watering.

For clarity, this is not the same Bobby Peel who was twice British prime minister, the one who modernised the coppers, who were thereafter named 'bobbies' after him. Our Bobby Peel played four decades later, though his infamous drinking probably meant he ran into some bobbies over the journey.

Bobby was one of those Yorkshire pros who had to do pretty much everything himself, with 1775 first-class wickets and more than 12,000 runs to his name, while the county often struggled. In Tests, his left-arm grenades made him the fifth bowler in the world to reach 100 wickets, though unlike those before him, Peel's whole tally came against Australia.

Part one of his trilogy saw Peel well watered by himself, and later by our old friend AE Stoddart. It was December 1894, Peel's seventh Ashes and fourth trip to Australia. England had won six of those series, and Bobby had enjoyed highlights like 5 for 18 in Adelaide, our number that led us to his story. By this stage the old stager was feeling himself, confident of his place, and started behaving like it, so much so that even the record-setting party boy Stoddy had to warn him to cut the booze or go home.

Boozed or no, the first Test in Sydney was extraordinary. Only four teams have won a Test after following on. Stoddy's team were the first and remained the only for 97 years. Australia made 586, followed by England's 325. These days no team would ever enforce the follow-on after 140 overs, but in that era Australia had already enjoyed a rest day, and a lot of players ambled up to bowl rather than expending too much energy.

England did better the second time around, making 437, but that only proved that the pitch was a belter. It was a timeless Test, so Australia had full leisure to make 177 to win. They knocked off 113 by stumps on day five, needing 64 the next morning with eight wickets in hand.

But this is Sydney, and one thing a Sydney summer does is rain. Abruptly and enthusiastically. That's what it did all night. And when those old pitches got soaked with water and then started to dry in the morning sun, the soil became crusty on top but moist underneath, creating divots that would harden, giving plenty of purchase and unpredictable bounce. This was the original meaning of 'sticky wicket': one that suddenly was a batting lottery.

Not that Bobby Peel knew; he was dead to the world. See, Bobby had been out on the lash. He had assumed the next day's play to be a formality, one that could be dispensed with by lesser bowlers. It certainly wasn't a situation that should keep him from plunging into a restorative ice bath full of beers.

In the morning, nobody could even find him. Was he asleep in a garden bed somewhere? Had he made new friends, hitched a ride to some far-flung house to keep carousing? A couple of teammates were also variously reported to be among the missing. The most popular story says that Bobby eventually arrived at the SCG so hungover that Stoddart stuck him in a cold shower for a long soak to wake him up. That may be embroidered, because there's no clear evidence of it, but here's the thing: if it isn't true, then Bobby must have been passed out for even longer. Because either way, he wasn't present and fit to play until close to lunchtime.

This does make you wonder. If England weren't ready, Australian captain Jack Blackham could have claimed a forfeit from the umpires. Perhaps not wanting to stoke discontent at the beginning of a series, he was polite enough to allow the late start. In the end, he should have been more ruthless. Because when Bobby did show, he found a surface tailored for his bowling, and smashed enough Berocca to shake off his dustiness and use it.

His final analysis was 6 for 67, but most of those runs had come the previous afternoon. The first five days had seen 32 wickets for 1478 runs; the last eight wickets on the final day fell for 36. The Aussie skipper had dropped himself to last man in, hardly able to hold the bat as he had a split thumb. 'But he had only made 2 when he spooned one from Peel back to the bowler who held it, took off his cap, and jumped for joy', said the news report. England had won by 10 runs.

It was the first stunner in a series that went on to offer more of the same. The next match was the one with Arthur Coningham's first-ball wicket and Stoddart's comeback hundred. England went 2–0 up, Australia fought the score back to 2–2, and with all eyes on the decider, England closed it out in a rare fifth Test that had everything on the line. This is where the full prestige of the Ashes was really born.

So we come to the second watering. WG Grace wasn't on that tour to Australia, but he was paying attention back home, and he took one lesson: get Peel on a wet track. Grace is feted as the godfather of English cricket, but being so good at the game also made him expect it to be played on his terms. He assumed the right to cheat when he couldn't tolerate the alternative, treating it as the universe correcting itself: popping bails back on, manipulating umpires, intimidating opponents, and indulging in a bit of light kidnapping when the moment arose.

It's no surprise that when Australia next toured in 1896, in another tied series with one match to play, having Grace in charge meant shenanigans were bound to be afoot. It was already a difficult pitch: England started with 145, Australia

119. But while it was expected to improve, the Australians got on top, getting England 5 for 60. With one day to go England led by 76, with the chance to add a few in the morning. On an easing pitch, Australia would have by far the better chance. But if the pitch got wrecked, England could crab to 80 or 90 in front and defend. And after two matches without him, Grace had picked Bobby Peel.

It was a wild coincidence that Australia should roll up on the final day to find that the drying pitch had been heavily watered overnight. A Test pitch is sacrosanct, untouched for the match's duration except for the roller and sweeping up debris. Nothing to the contrary would have happened without the direct order of someone as powerful as Grace. England's captain claimed that it had rained during the night – funny, given no meteorological service or casual observer had noticed a drop fall within miles of Vauxhall or Kennington.

Here's *Wisden*, with British understatement: 'It was freely predicted that the wicket would improve, but such was far from being the case, the pitch being perhaps more difficult than ever.' Deirdre Chambers, what a coincidence. There's at least a 50 per cent chance that Bobby Peel did not start the day quite as hungover this time, but either way, it didn't matter. He ended up with 111 to defend and didn't even need half that many, hoovering up 6 for 23 to win match and series.

The third watering, in Bobby's defence, was wildly misreported. In 1897, his drinking finally saw him sacked by Yorkshire, and a lot of enthusiastic retellings say that this became evident when he unzipped and hosed down the next few strips on the square. Cue the old line about having a slash outside the off stump. It's hard to think of a similar example: even England's Ashes players in 2013 waited until darkness fell and the crowd had left before turning The Oval into Splash Mountain.

We're sure this story about Bobby didn't actually happen, not just because it would be tough to unleash a litre of hot Foster's while going unnoticed by two umpires, two Middlesex batters, and an entire crowd of spectators, but also because it's easy to trace the misunderstanding. A newspaper writer decades later had reported the story as it was told to him by an elderly gent who had been a member of the crowd that day. The thing is, the gent didn't say that Bobby *had pissed on* the wicket but that Bobby *was pissed at* the wicket.

The latter rings true. Bobby was 40, and while still performing, had been pushing his luck for a long time. That previous Australia tour confirms the taking of liberties. On this day, Bobby opened the bowling, which was normal, and got dragged after seven overs, which wasn't. He later slipped twice in the field. His captain, Lord Hawke, had sacked a bunch of players a few years earlier for sauce-related reasons. Whether it was the bowling or the fielding, Lord Hawke had finally seen enough. Both the camel and Bobby Peel had received one straw too many.

Bobby later told a reporter that his bent spikes were to blame, and that he'd just had the modest regulation amount of breakfast gin. Funnily, he stayed suspended, and soon went off to play as a professional in league cricket instead. As far as history knows, he never did piss on anything important, so let's clear his name there. And as water runs downhill, Bobby eventually found his own level. He ended up running a pub, though we're not sure if they made any profit.

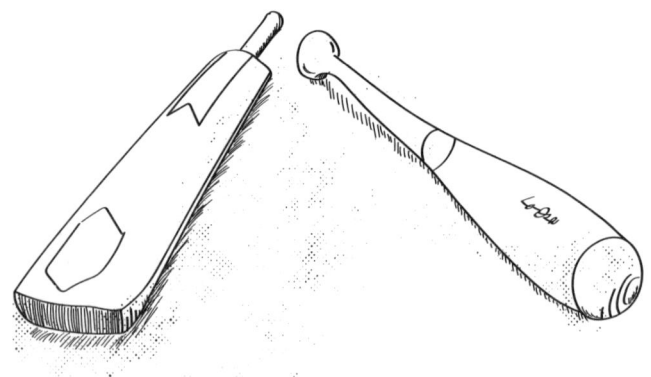

11

BRADMAN'S HONEYMOON

19.32

**Clue sent by:
David Jones**

'BRADMAN DOES NEW YORK' ISN'T EXACTLY A familiar strand of the sepia-toned nostalgia story. But it did happen, on a trip with a lot more besides.

We know the Don didn't mind making runs, we know he didn't mind making a quid, and we know he was up for an adventure. Put those together and you get the story born from our number, 19.32. An unusual clue from David Jones (the guy, not the shop) told us that in fact there was no right answer, and instead we should find one that suited us. We answered with the Australian winter of 1932, when instead of the familiar path to England, a tour headed to the USA and Canada.

This was very much a commercial tour, not an official team, but it did feature some Test players. Like the start of a good heist movie, retired leg spinner Arthur Mailey was the character tasked with pulling a squad together. Bradman was cricket's biggest star, and Mailey put the hard word on him, saying the whole thing would fall over if he wasn't involved.

One problem, Bradman pointed out, was that he was going to marry Jessie Menzies that April, and they had plans for the winter. Another was that he was due to start work for a newspaper and radio station – the same job that later cost him a Test during Bodyline. In response, on top of the £100 tour fee, Mailey offered to pay Don's salary for his time off work, plus – in the days when families never came on tour – expenses for the couple to travel together. Jessie had never left Australia, so she thought this a great deal: the cricket trip would also be their honeymoon.

An idiosyncratic bunch signed up alongside Don. Two young bucks: Stan McCabe was new in the Test team, Chuck Fleetwood-Smith yet to debut. Two current Test veterans: Vic Richardson (granddad to the Chappell brothers) and Alan Kippax. Two retirees: Mailey had finished for Australia six years earlier, still fresh next to wicketkeeper Sammy Carter, well into his 50s with a Test debut 25 years behind him. Then a step down to the rest of the squad: three with a sprinkle of state matches, including the unfortunately named Richard Nutt, and a couple of clubbies, spanning professions like doctor, lawyer, stockbroker. But hey, they still knew how to play better than Yanks or Canadians.

So began a truly bonkers itinerary: 51 matches in 20 towns across 76 days, a round trip of 10,000 kilometres, with only one spare player. A couple of matches were 11 versus 11, a couple were vaguely competitive, but for the most part – George Washington, your boys took a hell of a beating. The first game the tourists ransacked 503 from 368 balls before Mailey took nine wickets, and that pretty much set the tone.

Most often having a single day against teams of 15 to 20,

the Australian XI had to make enough runs to outweigh two opposition innings, plus take 28 to 38 wickets – and they *still* won four matches outright. They won 35 more on first-innings points, and four single-innings games. There were seven interrupted draws in strong positions. And there was one outlier, early in the tour, with a solitary 'loss' based on trailing the first innings by 18 runs. Bradman, it seems, was not happy. The same team played the next fixture, and he pumped them with 180.

That was one of his 16 hundreds on tour, out of 3777 runs at 102. McCabe made 2351 at 55. And it's safe to say that the Americas had not yet been sufficiently exposed to wrist spin. Bowling eight-ball overs, Fleetwood-Smith took 238 wickets at 7. Mailey, ostensibly the tour manager, took 203 at 8. Bradman barely used his leggies but rolled up one day against Vancouver to open the bowling. His first three overs got smashed, 1 for 43. His fourth over took 6 for 0.

They played everybody. From west coast to east, down into the States and back up north. They played city teams: Calgary, Toronto, Montreal, Detroit, Edmonton, Winnipeg. State teams: Illinois, New York, California. Regional teams: Western Ontario, Ottawa Valley. Boondocks teams: Saskatoon, Regina, Moose Jaw. They played a pretty solid West Indian team in Manhattan and jazz-hat teams like the Northern California All-Stars, who got bowled out for 20 and 33. At one point Mailey jumped ship to a British Columbia colts team, opening the batting for them, then swapped back the next day to take seven-for. It was fast, hectic, and loose as hell.

Getting whiplash following the itinerary, though, one thing comes to mind. The Don as an old gent was known as a sober and serious dude. But as a young man, you have to question his decision-making. A trip that lasts for 71 days, with 51 playing sport with a bunch of other blokes and presumably every other day travelling with them. That is the choice that Don and Jessie made. On. Their. Honeymoon.

We all know what activity honeymoons are meant to be for, especially back in the days when conservatism demanded saving oneself for marriage, and before most people even had their own car to host a bit of discreet hand stuff during the driveway drop-off. Honeymoons were the one time when starch-collared society said that you could flip release on that relationship pressure valve before going back to a life of repression. And while it will still be considered an offence against national sanctity to raise the image of the Bradmans on the job, you have to suggest that signing up for this schedule would have greatly impeded the primary point of the trip. Simply, when did they have time to bang it out?

Ah well. At least he got to meet Babe Ruth. A cool crossover, the cricketer and the baseballer who were both twice as good as anyone else in their sport, just shooting the breeze in New York City. 'Us little fellows could hit them harder than the big ones,' is the line attributed to the Babe, who was six-foot-two and a hundred kegs next to the Don at five-foot-seven. What the Babe really liked hearing was that in cricket, you don't have to run when you smash the ball. Imagine, slugging dingers without the trip round the bases.

Others were more satirical.

'Cricket is a nice way of demonstrating out in the fresh air and sunshine the astounding wizardry of British pantsmakers,' wrote the *New York Evening Post,* impressed at trousers that 'stay put without the boon of belts or galluses. You throw a red ball in the manner of a middle-aged pitcher on the Bloomer Girls' Baseball Team. The ball hits a green carpet something like the ones they spread on the steps at church weddings. If the batsman, who has shin-guards and a pleasant air, likes it, he swats it. If not, he turns his back on it. It's not as exciting as the recent Ocean City National Boys' Marbles Championship Contest; it's not as spectacular as watching the chaps dig the Rockefeller-Radio City foundations; but it is positively breathless compared with the subway ride up there to see it.'

Having gone from Vancouver to New York and back again, the Australians moved down into California, playing in San Francisco and Santa Barbara, before finishing with three matches against a Hollywood team and one against the marvellously named British Born Film Stars. The captain was Sir Charles Aubrey Smith, the venerable actor who decades earlier had toured Australia with Stoddy's proto-Lions rugby team, and had played one cricket Test in 1899.

In Hollywood, Smith was better known as the dad of Tarzan's girlfriend, but he top-scored against the Aussies with 24, and he had mates who wanted to play. Boris Karloff rocked up, fresh off playing Frankenstein's monster, and made 12. There was Murray Kinnell, who convinced Bette Davis not to quit acting, and Desmond Roberts, who was in her breakthrough film *Of Human Bondage*. There was James Finlayson, the comic foil for Laurel and Hardy, whose expostulations of dismay were the model for Dan Castellaneta when voicing Homer Simpson.

Smith's team got thumped, but this was the decisive moment that caused him to establish the famous Hollywood Cricket Club, which would start operations within a year. Smith convinced city authorities to give him a plot of land north of the Los Angeles River, at the fringes of sprawling Griffith Park, a mile or two over the mountain from the Hollywood sign, where he built his dream field and pavilion. Errol Flynn, David Niven, and PG Wodehouse were among those who turned out in the early days of the club, and a version of it carries on in a different location today. Like Wattle Flat, the original ground became an equestrian centre. There's always a horse willing to ruin our day.

So, the party sailed from San Francisco, and Bradman missed his only chance for a match in New Zealand when a game got rained off in Wellington. They got home later in 1932, shortly before a rather more intense series unfolded, when Douglas Jardine arrived with some fast bowlers and fun new tactics. Bradman's choices partly echo a later honeymoon story, when Indian legend Rahul Dravid married Vijeta Pendharkar in 2003, and Scotland were incongruously in an English domestic league. The Scots wanted Dravid, he wanted some UK batting, and it was a chance for a trip away. But, smart guy, he took a month off in the middle to enjoy some travel and a new marriage. We hope they had more fun than Don and Jessie.

12

BART KING AND THE GENTS OF PHILLY

10.53

**Clue sent by:
James Melinson**

AS WITH SEVERAL NUMBERS IN THIS BOOK, 10.53 instinctively feels like bowling figures. And it is Jim Laker's famous 10 for 53 against Australia, the best return in Tests. But that story is too obvious. First-class cricket offers another 10 for 53, and this one is off-Broadway, despite being closer to it.

Yes, we're going back to the USA. Not to New York City but a couple of hours down the road to Philadelphia. The spread of baseball plus a little tension over the American Revolutionary War kind of ruined cricket's chances in the States, and only recently has it taken tentative steps back towards prominence. But the home of cream cheese is also the city where the game has most determinedly hung on, even when it was in full retreat elsewhere.

In the late 1800s, when that retreat was deep, Philadelphia still had a quality cricket scene. Several clubs fed into a rep side, but rarely were they so plain as to just use the name of their city. No, with a sense of flair, they often went with 'the Gentlemen of Philadelphia'. That team had played in some capacity since the 1850s and staged an inaugural first-class match against a touring Australian team in 1878.

That's right, the 1932 trip was not the first Australian visit to the USA. Back in the early days, every Test tour was organised by players for coin, so it made sense to cap off a visit to England by going home via lucrative fixtures on the US east coast and the Panama Canal, rather than the Suez Canal and southern Asia. That means that 18 months after the first ever Test, the USA and Canada met a bunch of legendary names we've heard of: the Bannerman brothers, Fred Spofforth, Jack Blackham, Dave Gregory, Billy Murdoch. They mashed the other teams, but Philly took a first-innings lead, and it took a big intervention from Spofforth to set up an Australian win.

In 1893, the Australians returned, having lost the Ashes in England 1–0. No doubt they were tired after a long tour, but they wouldn't have expected a Gents side to come out swinging. And they weren't expecting to meet the greatest Gent of all, the man with the beautiful action and the serial-killer eyes. Here came John Barton King.

Tall and athletic, Bart King hadn't yet turned 20. He'd found cricket through baseball, and he looks like it. Photos of his bowling action show a gather with both hands clasped above his head, like a pitcher, but then it unfolds with elegance and power. The front arm takes a position to launch forward, letting the bowling arm whip through behind. And boy, did it work. He swung the ball late, at pace, in both directions: the holy trinity of swing.

When the Australians rocked up, they wouldn't have enjoyed conceding 525 in the first innings, but they would have expected to be able to bat a commensurate amount of time themselves. They wouldn't have expected a 19-year-old to knock over four of the top five and bowl 25 overs unchanged through the innings, finishing with 5 for 78. Bart had already notionally played for a USA team against Canada, but that was a two-dayer that was a glorified club match, so this was his first-class debut.

Behind by 326, the Australians followed on – and so did Bart, with a further 32 and a half overs. Fatigue dulled his returns with 2 for 90, but he'd given the Gents such a buffer that his teammates could make up the difference. In an all-time upset, a Test-strength Australian side was done by an innings and 68 runs by a team of American amateurs.

The Aussies won a return bout, and another team visited in 1896 to win a couple more, even though Bart was underbowled in the first match and kept knocking over the best players: Clem Hill, George Giffen, Joe Darling, Syd Gregory. In the third game of the second visit, he repeated his trick from three years earlier: 5 for 43 in the first innings, 3 for 47 in the third, setting up another Gents win by an innings.

Bart King was too good for club cricket. He once took 9 for 4 in a local match; two other times he took out the whole team. He took five wickets or more in an innings 177 times. With the bat, while his first-class scores tended to be useful rather than decisive, at lower levels he made 28 centuries, including a double and two triples. There was such a gulf between that level and the top, but living in the USA, there were only sporadic opportunities to show his stuff against the best.

When he did get the chance, he used it. The Gents visited

England in 1897, not with recognition as a national side but otherwise similar to an Australian tour, playing most counties plus MCC. Philly were outmatched but won the games when Bart took off: 12 wickets against Warwickshire, 13 against Sussex, when he rissoled the great Ranjitsinhji for a golden duck. He finished the tour with 72 wickets at 24, and two months later when Plum Warner led a reciprocal English side to Philadelphia, Bart welcomed them with 9 for 25.

Six years on, his next trip to England bagged another 78 wickets at 16, and the Gents became a force, beating six of the county sides. Against Lancashire, Bart once again took nine-for in one innings and 14 in the match. Against Surrey, run out for 98 in the first innings, he followed up with 113 not out in the second, his two best first-class scores in the same match.

Beating MCC in those days was the marker of cricket success, and he did that in Philly in 1905, then at Lord's in 1908, now contributing runs as an opening bat as well as his usual wickets. The 1908 tour was his best yet: across England and Ireland he cleaned up 87 wickets at 11 apiece.

Late in his career, that 10-wicket innings came round at first-class level. It was September 1909 when the Gentlemen of Ireland got the memo about naming conventions while touring Philadelphia. They didn't get the memo about Bart: seven bowled, two lbw, one catch. In a beautiful finishing touch, the not-out batter was the opener, who had carried his bat for an even 50 runs. But to start the innings, Bart had bowled him off a no ball. Bart King may be the only bowler to have actually knocked over all 11 players in a side.

By the end Bart was nearly 40, but it didn't matter. It was 1912 when he finished as he'd started 19 seasons earlier, against the Australians. After a mid-range Gents score, he took 5 for 40 to turn that into a lead. After a third-innings Gents collapse, he knocked the top off the innings to start defending 138. With the Aussies needing 16 to win, 8 down, he came back to bowl the last two players and win by 2 runs. It should have started a clean sweep: the second and final game, he chipped in 5 for 22, a score of 45 and 3 for 52, but his team failed to chase 127.

Still, he couldn't have done much more – the story of his career. Limited to 65 first-class matches, Bart King took 415 wickets at the stunning average of 15.65. If he'd been from a Test country he would be revered as one of the greats. But we doubt it bothered him any. Numbers are numbers, but he was renowned as a storyteller and joke spinner, was happily married for 50 years, lived to just short of his 92nd birthday, and remains the greatest American cricketer of all time.

13

ABSOLON, ABSOLOM

5.19

Clue sent by:
Nick Dempsey

A lot of our Nerd Pledge numbers in this book have related to bowling figures. So, surprise! This number is also about wickets. But it's not about somebody taking 5 for 19. It's about taking 519 wickets ... in a single season.

First, some clarity: we're talking about Charlie Absolon, not Charlie *Absolom*. One letter makes a difference. Absolom, the latter, played a Test in 1879, the match in Melbourne just before the Sydney Riot. The following year, he vanished from England. Next anyone heard was a decade later, when he died in Trinidad. Loading a ship, he was, most reports claim, crushed by a load of bananas. Better research suggests a load of sugar. Either way, it was a sticky ending.

But that's not our guy. Charlie Absolom, Test cricketer, was born in 1846. Charlie Absolon, Swiss Army knife cricketer, was much older, born in 1817. But he still outlasted the other Charlie by 20 years, living to 90 and spending most of that time on a cricket field.

Born in Oxfordshire, our Charlie started club cricket at 14 and retired at 80. Unlike most names in this book, he had no international or first-class career, but he played every other kind of match he could find. He was always fit, he was obsessed with the sport, and he turned out for dozens of clubs, begging for a game anywhere one was played, even turning out two or three times on the same day.

The thing is, thanks to 1800s paperwork, we have no statistical record of the first 37 years of his career. The details only begin from 1868, when he was already 51 years old. So, strap yourself in. From the ages of 51 to 80, Charlie Absolon played 30 seasons, made 26,000 runs, and took 8500 wickets, including *59 hat-tricks*.

It's hard to know where to start with this guy. A butcher by trade, as a younger man he became prominent in a labour-rights campaign to legislate a Saturday half-day off for recreation. No prizes for guessing why he wanted the extra time. He cajoled his workmates into forming a team called the United Master Butchers (read it back twice to be sure). That way there was always a game to be had.

Absolon was a decent bat, making his first century at 15, and a famed slip catcher, able to pluck just about anything that came by. But his main game was with the ball. In the style of the era of his youth, he bowled underarm lobs, but he was bloody good at them, mixing up pace and making the ball turn. Lob bowling fell out of fashion, and people scoffed at the old duffer still sending it down – until he got them out, as he eventually did to everybody he came up against. The season with 519 wickets came when he was 55 years old, but he had lots of other seasons in the multiple hundreds.

Have a look at some of Charlie's ways to dominate a game. Several times he took all 10 wickets himself. Across two innings for Wood Green in 1872, he took 18 wickets and held the catches for the other two. In a match in 1884, when his opponents needed three runs to win with five wickets in hand, Absolon promptly knocked over all five in six balls.

For his beloved United Master Butchers, against a Metropolitan Clubs team with 20 players, Charlie took the first 18 wickets out of 19, bowling out the opposition for 4. Yes, for 4.

In a beautiful crossover of stories, at the age of 51, Charlie played against the touring Aboriginal team of 1868 – not once, but twice. First he turned out for the Gentlemen of Middlesex, then for the Gentlemen of Surrey. Was he really part of either county? No. So why did that happen? Because why not? It's Charlie Absolon. He does what he wants.

In 1873, he played a much-promoted exhibition game as part of a team of 12, taking on the three best cricketers in the country: WG Grace, Walter Gilbert, and Harry Charlwood. Given the mismatched numbers, the rules were that scoring had to come in boundaries and only in front of square. The three champions, all aged between 20 and 25, bowled out the dozen challengers for 15 runs. But Charlie Absolon, at 56 years old, bowled out the superstars to win in 19 balls.

Our favourite part of the story is in 1875 when, at a sprightly 58, he lined up for county-affiliated duty again. Which team? Middlesex Young Cricketers, taking on the Surrey Young Cricketers. Criminally, despite an extended team list, they didn't let him have a bowl and batted him at number 13. So he finished not out in both innings and took three catches. You can't keep Charlie out of a game.

On and on he went across the years. In a dozen of his final 30 seasons, he topped both 200 wickets and 1000 runs. One account has him playing against four generations of the same family. Long before the exhibition match with Grace, he had played against all of the Grace brothers as schoolboys, and the year he died was the year that WG retired after 44 seasons. Charlie had played 66.

In his final season, he had to bat with a runner and could only field at slip, but he was still grabbing chances and still bowling his lobs. He took over 100 wickets that season at *80 fucking years old*. He was Charlie Absolon: the most can't-stop, won't-stop cricketer of all time.

14

CHARLES PALMER AND THE WET PATCH

3.74

**Clue sent by:
Angus Digby**

Sometimes, a list of cap numbers is all you need to lead to the weird and wonderful. Charles Palmer was England cap 374, not that he knew it at the time, and not that he was expecting to play the one Test of his career. Palmer was from the Midlands and went to Birmingham University, but played as an amateur, which was unusual given that most of those tended to be Oxford or Cambridge types. Being born just after one World War, he managed two seasons with Worcestershire before losing six years to the next one, manning an anti-aircraft battery in Sussex.

Palmer meandered from the war into teaching and played first-class cricket here and there, deep into his 20s. But when Bradman's Invincibles toured in 1948, he carved 85 runs in a morning off Keith Miller, Ray Lindwall, and the rest for his county. With MCC wanting to broaden the type of people declaring as amateurs, he was picked to tour South Africa, and while he didn't play a Test, he was there for the whole English winter and apparently had the time of his life.

In 1950, Palmer switched to Leicestershire, not only as captain but also club secretary. This paid gig allowed him to keep playing, which was how so many supposed amateurs worked around the reality of making a living. The secretary had a broad job, so Palmer was responsible for organising not just the team on the field and the social activities off it, but the fundraising efforts: the football pools, the chicken dinners – all the daily mundanities of running a club.

The dual roles worked, because he hit his straps: four seasons from 1950 to 1953 with 15 centuries and over 7000 runs, including a big fourth-innings hundred at Lord's when the amateur Gentlemen missed out by two runs against the professional Players. Perennial battlers Leicestershire finished third in 1953. That's how he ended up on the West Indies tour of 1953/54, as much for his performance as an administrator as a player.

This also reflects some dodgy dealings: the West Indies refused to pay travel costs for a tour manager, so England claimed that Palmer was their 16th player while slotting him into the other job. MCC didn't trust Len Hutton as a professional player to captain without some stiff-upper-lip amateur to watch over him. As it turns out, it was a wild time geopolitically: Caribbean countries were breaking away from UK rule, and the ill-tempered tour featured racism, riots, threats, and violence, in what was ultimately a diplomatic debacle.

Charles Palmer was in the midst of it, and opinions differ on whether he was up to the task. They also differ on why, before the second Test at Barbados, Hutton decided that Palmer should play. Palmer had turned out in one tour match and hadn't picked up a bat in a month. But he came in at number six, making 22 and 0 in a big defeat. That was it for his Test career.

His first-class career offers a far stranger, scarcely believable story. Palmer was a short guy, balding, bespectacled, unimposing in any physical sense. His contemporary Trevor Bailey described him as 'a hen-pecked bank clerk in a farce'. In 1955, he led Leicestershire at home against Surrey, and this Surrey team was perhaps the best of the lot in their era of all-time dominance, squarely in the middle of winning seven County Championship titles in a row. They had the famed spin pair Tony Lock and Jim Laker, one of England's greatest seamers in Alec Bedser, and powerful batting in every position. In this match, as per their standard, they bowled out Leicestershire for 114.

Surrey's reply was cruising at 1 for 42, their best bat in Peter May at the crease, when Palmer brought himself on for an over to swap ends for his spinners. He asked May to go easy on him, saying he hadn't bowled all year. This was almost true – he'd bowled in two games and totalled four overs. Now, let's not claim he wasn't a bowler: he was useful enough for 365 career wickets at better than one per match, averaging 25. But he wasn't a frightening option. His party trick was the donkey drop, hurling the ball 20 feet in the air to land on top of the stumps. The rest of the time, it was gentle mediums.

On this day, he'd noticed a wet patch on the pitch at Grace Road, so he thought he would try hitting it to see if the ball would skid.

Over an hour later, his one over had become a dozen. The scoreboard read 12 overs, 12 maidens, 8 for 0. Against the best team in the land by the length of the Flemington straight, Palmer had knocked over eight of them, seven of them bowled, without conceding a run. Hit the wet patch, hit the stumps, again and again and again.

This created an interesting dynamic when it came to what happened next. The best first-class analysis for eight wickets was 8 for 2, and that record belonged to Laker. Laker was the man at the non-striker's end as Palmer took his seventh wicket, then his eighth. The last pair came together. For Palmer's next over, Laker was on strike, with the fate of his own record in his hands. He played. He miscued. *He was dropped.*

Admittedly, the catch would also have saved Laker's eight-wicket record, because Palmer should have had 9 for 0. But once the catch had gone down, Laker needed to take the bowler for runs. He swung the bat hard, he got lucky, and he slashed away a three and a four before being bowled by the bloke at the other end. Palmer finished with 14 overs, 12 maidens, 8 for 7. Figures ruined.

On a roll, Palmer went on to top-score in the third innings with 64, but Surrey chased 203 easily to win. Did he give himself another spell? You bet he did. This time, Surrey played him with complete caution. Palmer didn't get a wicket, but his 13 overs conceded one run. That made match figures of 27 overs, 24 maidens, 8 for 8, and his side had still been pumped. Ever the gent, Palmer popped into the Surrey rooms to acknowledge the feat with, 'Sorry, gentlemen!'

Later, he would be chair of Leicestershire, then MCC president, all five-foot-seven of him lining up against Kerry Packer during the World Series Cricket war. He chaired the English board in the 1980s and pushed two big ideas. The first, changing county cricket to four-day matches, they took on. The second, going back to uncovered pitches, they did not. But how else are you supposed to take 8 for 7? Still fourth on the eight-wicket record list and always cap 374, Charles Palmer is a classic Dusty Old Bastard.

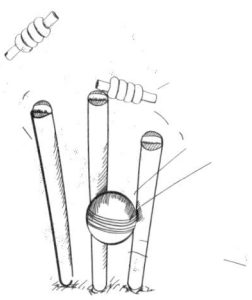

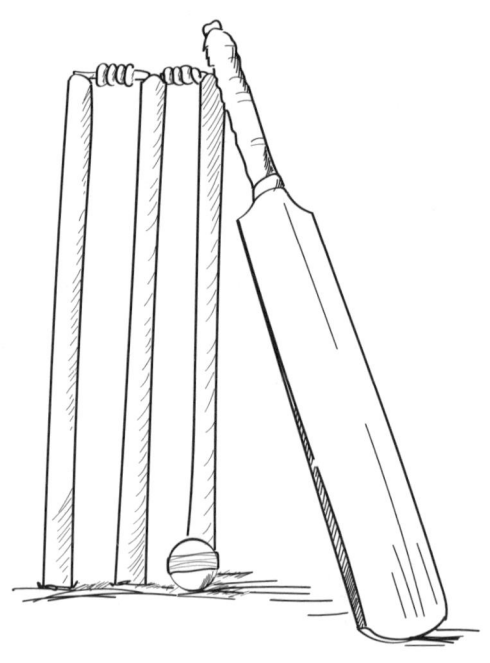

15

CRAWLING TO THE WICKET

2.50

**Clue sent by:
Chris Arkle**

IN THE 1890S, THERE WERE ENOUGH SONS OF dead doctors knocking about that someone set up an entire school for sons of dead doctors. That's how Harold Heygate came to play for Epsom College, then county cricket for Sussex. So began, in 1903, a cricket career that was simultaneously very long, very short, and very strange.

His brother Reggie was already playing for Sussex and would do so for 10 years. Harold, at 18 years old, joined in for two games in the middle order, didn't make many, and was dropped. It took two more years to get his next shot: usually an opening bat, by 1905 he was now in his preferred spot. He knocked up 40 and 24, top score and second-top score as they won a thriller, then 80 and 68 not out, top score and second-top score in a huge win. Next time he missed out, 0 and 2, in an inconsequential university match that Sussex won anyway.

And ... that was that. Ten days in June, three games, 250 runs to reflect our Nerd Pledge number, and punted, in one of the most nonsensical bits of sporting selection you're likely to see. It's not like Sussex had a hot option burning to take the opener's spot: they tried a mediocre all-rounder named

Charles Smith, got mediocre returns from all-rounder Albert Relf, and by season's end had stuck their best player, CB Fry, back up there to plug the gap. And yet, our mate Harold wouldn't appear on a first-class scorecard again for 14 years.

Whether that was the cause or not Harold buggered off, seemingly to North America, as he popped up on scorecards for Ottawa and for Canada between 1907 and 1909. Then he went to war. British service records are often inaccessible or incomplete, so the best we can deduce is that Harold got some sort of leg injury late in World War I and persistently suffered from rheumatism, a painful swelling of the joints, worsened by trench life. He made his way home, damaged but alive.

Cricket had been on hiatus, but with the Armistice in 1918, there was a push to organise a season for 1919. The urge was to get back to something approaching normal life as quickly as possible, to help heal the horrors of the preceding four years. The problem was that so many men had been killed and so many others injured that it was hard to field a qualified team. Those who had survived were still scattered all round the theatres of combat, and those who'd enlisted wouldn't be demobilised for up to a year, and some even longer.

Counties had to cast around, seeking anyone in reasonable condition who knew their way round bat and ball. Sussex would field 36 players that season, still a club record. And ahead of their season opener against Somerset, the situation was especially acute. When they spotted Harold Heygate in the stands at Taunton, there as a spectator, they asked him to fill the last spot in the XI.

Now, Harold was approaching 35 and was clearly in bad shape from the war, but in a time of need, he agreed. He wasn't physically fit to field, which was surely self-evident, but Sussex evidently preferred to choose somebody with a link to the club rather than plucking someone at random from the crowd.

So began, years after his fifth, Harold's sixth and final first-class match – and weirdly, his third against local rivals Somerset. This scorecard has a couple of magnificent names, like Arthur Plantagenet Francis Cecil Somerset, who we hope was named after his club, and Sussex's Robert Alexander Tamblyn Miller, who comes up as RAT Miller. Cheese and whiskers, B1.

Somerset made 243 and Harold didn't field. But when Sussex replied with 242, Harold batted as last man in, scoring no runs but enabling the partnership that let George Cox get them within a run of parity.

Even that was too much of a strain. When the second day dawned, Harold had accepted the reality of his condition and given up any expectation of playing. He rolled up at the ground in civvies, wearing a blue suit. And indeed, it didn't seem that he was needed, sitting out the fielding portion as Somerset got rolled for 103, that man Cox with nine for the match. Sussex needed 105 to win.

Their skipper, Herbert Wilson, did his job at the top, but wickets kept falling at the other end. They went 4 for 39, 5 for 48, 6 for 48, before Henry Roberts joined Wilson and doused the fire. A partnership of 55 left two runs to win. Then at 6 for 103, Roberts was bowled for 28. Next ball, George

Stannard, also bowled, golden duck. With the strike back in the following over, Wilson scored a single. Scores were level, with wicketkeeper RAT Miller on strike ... but the RAT put his head in a trap. Caught for nought, off Somerset captain Jack White. The hardest little button to button.

From the brink of victory, Sussex had lost 3 for 1 and were nine wickets down. With Harold having been watching from the bench seats the whole day, the umpires moved to end the match.

But a shout went up from the pavilion. The players paused. The umpires waited.

Out came Harold, stumbling down the steps. He was still in his blue suit but was strapping batting pads over the top. He wasn't a fast mover, and there was a general fumbling with kit as he tried to get ready to take the field. With a few minutes passing, Somerset players started to complain, and, turning to the umpires, captain Jack White appealed.

He wasn't appealing for 'timed out' specifically, because that form of dismissal didn't exist yet, but players taking longer than two minutes to take guard could be simply recorded as absent, whether it counted as a wicket or not. At Taunton in May 1919, White asked the umpires to make that call, and they did. Sussex were nine down, all out, for 104, and the game was a tie.

Asked for clarification in the ensuing days, MCC said that the decision was correct under the Laws. But – in a classic letter versus spirit situation – the perception that Somerset had disrespected an injured war veteran was greeted with dismay. Newspapers said that the locals should have given Harold whatever time needed to get to the crease, given he was game enough to come out and play. *Wisden* had the same attitude: 'Whether or not Heygate would have crawled to the wicket, it was very unsportsmanlike that such a point should have been raised when there remained ample time to finish the match'.

Nobody has yet been timed out in a Test. But the risk is why a padded-up Nathan Lyon hobbled through the pavilion to wait for the next wicket near the boundary after he blew up his calf at Lord's in 2023. Angelo Mathews did cop one three months later during that year's World Cup, when he wandered off to get a new helmet before having taken guard. Given he hadn't asked if anyone minded, Bangladesh got tired of waiting. As much as Sri Lanka complained, the umpires had warned him time was short. Unlike Harold, he had two working legs.

Less debatable was Vasbert Drakes' dismissal in 2002. He'd been in Sri Lanka at the Champions Trophy playing for West Indies, so when he was due to bat for Border against Free State in South African domestic cricket, he was still on a flight halfway between the countries. Hard to argue that one, but Big Ange would have given it a shot.

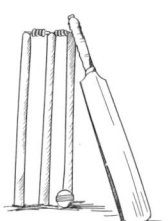

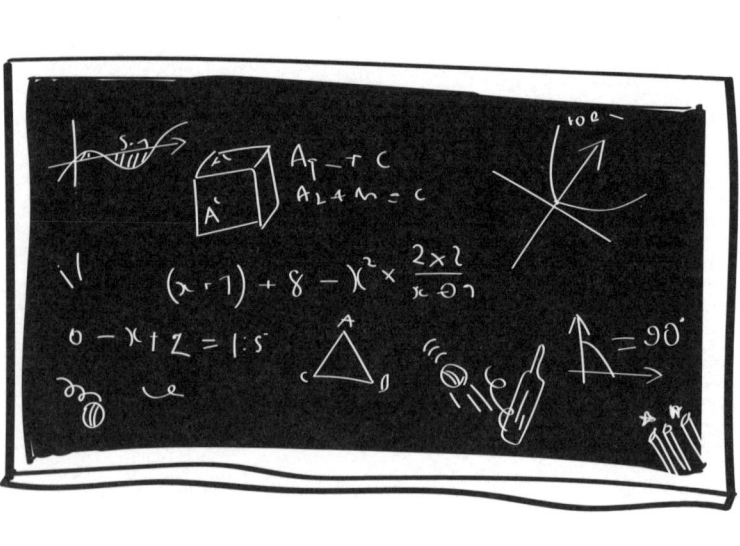

16

THE WAIKIKI FORMULA

22.13

Clue sent by:
Monique Beedles

OUR CLUE FOR THIS NUMBER MENTIONED a non-player who still influenced cricket, and that 'while they added a lot to the game, they could also divide'. Eventually we twigged: mathematics. Two mathematicians in particular have decided more matches than any player: Frank Duckworth and Tony Lewis. And the clue had arrived shortly after Frank died in 2024.

He was born in 1939 on Boxing Day, a great early cricket connection. Studying at the University of Liverpool, he stayed with a woman whose other lodger was her nephew, a young musician named John Lennon. 'I only exchanged words with him once,' was Frank's recollection. 'I said, "Hello John," and he said, "Um." I heard him playing a few chords in his bedroom occasionally.'

Frank studied physics, then a PhD in metallurgy, and ended up working on nuclear power in the labs of the Central Electricity Generating Board. Energy production generated a sea of data, and in essentially a pre-computer age, Frank turned out to be bloody good at drawing valuable information from it. 'With about 400 graduates and PhDs in the whole of the CEGB research department, there was hardly anyone who had studied statistics, so here was a subject to make my own.' He turned his training in that direction and joined the Royal Statistical Society.

Frank didn't mind a big project. He designed the International Nuclear and Radiological Event Scale, which ranks nuclear industrial accidents logarithmically, like the Richter scale. Later, as a hobby, he crunched the stats of every recorded means of death, allowing him to work out their relative risk. When you hear someone tell a nervous flyer that it's more dangerous to take a taxi to the airport than to get on the plane, that's based on Duckworth's research.

The Central Electricity Generating Board was chopped up in 1990, one of Margaret Thatcher's last gasps before being rolled as prime minister. Duckworth retired early from the private company that replaced it in 1992. He was 52 years old, brain firing and time on his hands, and it was a World Cup year.

During a wet tournament in Australia and New Zealand, rain delays used the 'most productive overs' method: if a team bowled 50 overs but would only get 40 to face, their target would be the combined runs from the first team's best 40 overs. The theory was that a shorter innings let the chasing team be more aggressive and forego the other team's conservative patches.

It made sense at a glance, but cricket doesn't work that neatly: bowlers can create low-scoring overs even in a short chase. And a bigger flaw was that this method made some sense when applied to the start of a chase, but not near the end of one. Back after their apartheid ban, the South Africans had a dynamic and popular team in their semifinal against England. Needing 22 runs to win with 13 balls remaining, there was a short rain delay. Officials had to reduce the overs by two, and the target by England's two lowest-scoring overs. But England had faced several maidens, so the run deduction was 0. Scoring 22 from 13 balls was tricky, but 22 from one ball was impossible. Hence our Nerd Pledge number of 22.13.

Listening to *Test Match Special* on the radio, Frank Duckworth could not let this statistical monstrosity stand:

> I distinctly remember the commentator, Christopher Martin-Jenkins, saying that surely someone, somewhere, could come up with something better! Then he read out some letters he had received making various suggestions and I remember thinking that every one of these was unsatisfactory in some way or other. Nobody seemed to realise that it was a mathematical two-factor problem and it needed a mathematical solution.

The hottest ticket in town was an invitation to the Royal Statistical Society conference, and Frank came up with a winning title for his paper: 'A Fair Result in Foul Weather'. That laid down his concept: that wickets remaining and overs to bat were resources available to the batting side, so you could work out a likely volume of scoring based on the intersection of those resources.

That gave three possibilities. For a team cut off batting first, extrapolating what they would likely have made in the full innings. For a team chasing with reduced overs, assessing a fair target across the overs they would get. And for chases cut off, assessing the likelihood of a successful chase from that position. If the same number of overs will likely yield more runs for a team two wickets down than for a team six wickets down, then the team six down needs to be that many runs closer to the target when the match is called off.

Frank's first shot didn't work because it was based on 'cricket intuition' rather than concrete numbers, but the paper tickled the attention of another mathematically minded cricket nuffy, Tony Lewis at the University of the West of England. It turned out they lived five miles apart in Lancashire, both club cricketers still turning out once in a while on weekends, but they had never met. Lewis punted the project to one of his students but kept being drawn back to the problem himself. Eventually he hit on extracting data from historical scoresheets and applying the formula to that. Using every previous result helps work out the most likely one today.

Duckworth and Lewis met in January 1995, when correspondence became friendship. They kept tinkering with the formula and sounding out the English board about its potential, but knew they hadn't perfected it. That was until late that year, when Frank Duckworth took a holiday to Hawaii. These things can happen as minds turn over on a long flight: among the dull roar of midair engines and plastic-wrapped cutlery, something clicked. He thought he had finally cracked the part that had been eluding them.

We like to think of Frank's wife in this situation. Picture it: a proper, sensible, retired British mathematician, reaching an island paradise to see sunlight for the first time in years, pulling up at the hotel from the airport, and instead of arranging his flip-flops in colour order and putting on a plush robe, he rushes into the office to breathlessly ask if they have a fax machine. Hopefully holding a folder spilling over with loose papers. This was 1995 – nobody was going to fire off an email. Phone calls would have cost the same as a Concorde ticket. The idea spilling out of his head had to be done right now. So day one of Frank's holiday was spent faxing back and forth, Tony at home and Frank annoying the hotel manager, finessing the final structure. By the time cocktail hour rolled around, it was done.

This was what they now presented with confidence to England's cricket authorities. We all came to know it as the Duckworth–Lewis method, while later when Australian statistician Steven Stern's contribution was added, it gave us the modern shorthand of DLS. But being modest mathematical types, this was not the name that the inventors proposed. They didn't think about citing themselves. In a meeting of science and art, their title was straightforward and logical but with an inadvertent dash of romance and flair. For all these years, whenever a game was shortened, we could have been saying, 'Time to apply the Waikiki Formula.'

Surely we can bring that back? Anyway, English cricket chief executive Tim Lamb took the Duckworth–Lewis method to an

ICC meeting chaired by West Indies legend Clyde Walcott and got permission to trial it. It was first used on New Year's Day 1997. With Zimbabwe out for 200 hosting England, the target became 186 when England's innings was reduced to 42 overs. Zimbabwe kept them to 7 for 179, the first Waikiki winners. The method was accepted for the 1999 World Cup, though it wasn't needed with reserve days available.

Duckworth and Lewis kept updating the formula, but the 2003 World Cup showed it breaking down with higher scores: anything over 300 tended to result in targets that were too low. They shifted to computer calculations rather than a paper table, which made the system more complex to use and is why these days nobody normal knows how it works, while a room of custodians behind the scenes quietly hand down the findings like a conclave of cardinals. Duckworth and Lewis had retired from handling the formula by 2014, and over the next 10 years both passed away. They handed it over to Stern to keep adjusting where required.

Mostly, the Waikiki Formula holds up. Twenty-over cricket is more likely to distort it, but especially in one-day cricket and in close finishes, people with cricketing sense generally agree that the result feels intuitively pretty right. If you go back and apply the formula to that 1992 semifinal, South Africa would have needed 4 to win from that last ball. They might have got it, they might not, just the same as they might not have got 22 from 13. But if you'd offered that target from one ball, both sides would probably have accepted it as a reasonable offer. Statisticians can't ask for better than that.

17

JOINING THE 400 CLUB

48.50

**Clue sent by:
Simon Wallace**

THE NUMBER 48.5 SOUNDS LIKE A BATTING average, and it turns out that it was, but only for one player: somebody who reached that mark in two Test matches yet never played a third. But an even stranger number than 48.5 in Aftab Baloch's career is 428: the Pakistani bat was overlooked for his country despite doing nothing wrong in his scant Test appearances and despite being one of nine players so far in first-class history to make a quadruple century.

We've talked about a few of these. First, boo, Archie MacLaren's 424, beaten twice by Bill Ponsford's 429 and 437. Don Bradman pipped Ponsford with 452. In 1948, with BB Nimbalkar on 443 not out, the opposing captain forfeited and abandoned the match rather than let him pass Bradman, so that was left to Hanif Mohammad in 1959, run out for 499.

Our man Aftab didn't threaten the record with 428, nor did Graeme Hick getting declared on with 405, but Brian Lara took it with 501, then backed that up 10 years later with the Test record of 400 even. In Gold FM style, that was one per decade in the 1970s, 80s, 90s, and 2000s. In the two decades since Lara we've only added Sam Northeast with 410 not out.

Aftab Baloch had pedigree. His dad, Shamsher Baloch, was in the 1940s generation that played Ranji Trophy in India before partition, then Quaid-e-Azam Trophy in Pakistan in the 50s. Once, he even turned out for the Indian state of Maharashtra, and after bowling out the oppo late in the day, Shamsher was sent out to open the batting as a nightwatchman – with who else but with BB Nimbalkar, before BB had joined the 400 Club.

Shamsher had two sons who played first-class cricket, but they were an exercise in contrast. Karimullah's record was shithouse: no wickets, six hits, 14 career runs. Aftab was a prodigy. Born on April Fools' Day, like David Gower, he was initially seen as an off spinner. In the summer of 1969, whether or not he got his first real six-string, he did get his first-class debut. He was 16 years old when the Public Works Department rocked up and said, 'Hey, want a job?' This was because the Public Works Department had a cricket team. Getting picked also meant getting employed.

Their scouting was spot-on. So you had a teenager on debut batting down at number nine, and what did he do? Walked in and made 77 not out, taking his side to a declaration at 452. Was he done? Tired? Ready to eat some cornflakes and watch *Ninja Turtles* and tell you to get out of his room and stop ruining his life? No, he turned around and took 6 for 33 to bowl out the other lot for 95. And when they followed on, another 6 for 46. So, a dozen wickets for the match plus an unbeaten fifty. Welcome.

From here, the young man went on a tear. Promoted

to number six against Kalat, he made 100 not out as they declared with over 500, then four wickets after the follow-on. His third game, promoted again to five against Quetta, Aftab tonned up once more, 104 as the side racked up 714. His fourth game, an important 25 not out to shore up a collapse, then 3 for 36 to ensure first-innings points. And against Sargodha, he top-scored with 120, took 3 for 31, added 51 not out, then presumably got a rest under child-labour laws as Public Works bowled their way to a win.

Aftab and company charged to the Quaid-e-Azam final, his sixth game of first-class cricket. For the first time, he went badly: wicketless while making 2 and 8. In the timeless grudge match, Public Works went down against Pakistan International Airlines, the glamorous internationalists of the comp, the flyboys who really crack you up. Still, the kid had made an impression, and New Zealand were about to hit town.

After a few runs and a wicket against the Kiwis in a warm-up, Aftab Baloch got picked for the third Test. At 16 years and 221 days, he was the second-youngest Test player behind his countryman Mushtaq Mohammad, and has only been passed since by Sachin Tendulkar, Mohammad Sharif, and Hasan Raza.

In contrary fashion, they picked him but barely used him. Final Word fave Glenn Turner always loved batting forever (a Glennternity?), so he went long and his teammates tried to match him, though everyone forgot about scoring runs. In 166.3 overs of grind, Aftab wasn't given a trundle. Three specialist spinners bowled 134 of those overs, while he was now regarded as a batter and listed at five. He made a useful

25 in a partnership of 69 on the way to a Pakistan lead and finally got to bowl two overs when the draw was all but done.

Our lad had acquitted himself well enough, but with terrible timing. Pakistan wouldn't play another Test for a year and a half. An under-25s trip to England got cancelled, and by the time the senior team made the same trip in 1971, a batting core had solidified made of revered Pakistan names: the great Zaheer Abbas, Majid Khan, Asif Iqbal, Wasim Raja, and Hanif Mohammad's brothers Mushtaq and Sadiq. Still a teenager, Aftab couldn't get a chance. He described it as heartbreaking.

He responded by doing the thing players are told to do: make bulk runs at domestic level. He averaged 49 or better for seven home seasons running, with 14 hundreds. He played against a decent Rest of the World team in 1973, dismissed once in four innings, then toured Sri Lanka, not yet a Test nation, and carved a big unbeaten hundred in a win. And in February 1974, our moment came.

Aftab had moved teams by then, becoming a first-class captain at 20 years old. He was batting for Sind against Baluchistan, as per their contemporary spellings, when he came to the crease at 2 for 116 having already rolled the opposition for nothing much. He batted to stumps on 44 not out, then all through day two for 326 not out. He might have declared, but young teammate Mohammad Akram was a stat rabbit and pointed out the rarity of players reaching 400. Only halfway through the four allotted days, so went the skipper, finally reaching nine and three-quarter hours at the crease.

Which brings us to one important point. Aftab Baloch only hit 25 fours in his entire innings, less than a quarter of his total. Depending how generously we fill in some scorecard gaps, the 284 runs scored by his partners would have contained between 20 and 30 more. This means that out of 712 runs scored while he was in the middle, this absolute maniac *ran* over 500 of them himself, some 70 per cent of the total, then later said that he was pleased that bad fielding gave him the chance to push for threes.

The last partnership was with a 16-year-old in his first season who Aftab had backed: a young Javed Miandad made the first century of a career that would end with 80 of them. With 951 on the board and Baluchistan bowled out a second time, the margin was an innings and 575 runs – the sixth biggest ever. Aftab, as urged by his teammate, had the sixth quadruple century.

But the match was in the margins of the margins. It wasn't televised, it wasn't taped, and as per Aftab's recollection, there wasn't even a photograph. There was no explosion of coverage, just a match report. A season worth 1205 runs did get him into the Pakistan squad for England later in 1974, but he was never in favour, and played a smattering of festival matches without notable success. Only after another bumper domestic season, with 1109 runs at 65 plus 40 wickets at 21, did national selectors pick him again.

By then it was February 1975, and the West Indies were the visitors. In the early days of their all-pace style, the bombardment came from Andy Roberts, Vanburn Holder,

Bernard Julien, and Keith Boyce. Aftab got bounced out for 12, then didn't bowl, as Pakistan made 199 and the Windies 214. In the third innings, with Pakistan five down and 199 in front, further wickets would have given up the match. Aftab dug in to support Mushtaq, then opened up. Second best on the card with 60 not out, he took Pakistan to safety with a chance at a win. West Indies had to dig in for a draw.

And that was that. On a Karachi flat-top, Pakistan mystifyingly went for an additional fast bowler, who got smashed around at 4.5 an over, before another 18-month gap between Tests. By October 1976, when the next match finally came around, that kid Javed Miandad was on debut. Tours came and went but there was no call-up for Aftab. Political influence and rivalries, rarely far away in Pakistan cricket, were likely a factor.

Aftab played another 10 domestic seasons up to 1985, treated badly by selectors in Pakistan but still bossing it at home. He was born in '69, had a debut partnership of 69 and died at 69, during the pandemic of 2022. His Test average suggests he deserved better, but his top score will keep him in rare company. Everybody needs a teammate who is a stats nerd.

18

FRANK THE TANKED

8.41

**Clue sent by:
Steve Dodkin**

Frank Ryan had a lot going on: A mysterious beginning with two birthplaces, a winding trail through five countries, a hot temper, a powerful thirst, two world wars, and a thousand first-class wickets after the age of 30.

We have consensus on a birthdate: Francis Peter Ryan, 14th of November, 1888. But at the time of writing, Cricinfo still has him born in New Jersey, USA, while others have him born in Uttar Pradesh, India. Then there's the matter of his cricket record, which the more readily available sources have as non-existent – not a school match, not a club match, not a hit on the beach – until his first-class debut in 1919.

Luckily some more detail is being unearthed, largely through Glamorgan club historian Andrew Hignell: most notably, solving the birth mystery. Frank was indeed born in Tundla, a small railway junction town near Agra, close to the Taj Mahal, where his Irish dad worked after joining the British Army. But in Frank's 20s, as an illegal migrant in New York City, he faked evidence that he was born in America so he could get free passage from Canada to England as a Commonwealth volunteer to enlist for World War I.

It had already been a varied life. He went to St Joseph's College in the Himalayas, then back to England as a teenager with his mother. He had in fact played school cricket, per some well-buried scorecards from a Calcutta newspaper, and was a good enough left-arm spinner to be used as a net bowler at The Oval and Lord's, at one point bowling the great CB Fry and winning interest from Gloucestershire. But his father had made him promise not to pursue cricket as a career, so he trained as an engineer, spent some time in Scotland, then worked on steamships going back and forth to New York.

New York was where he might, in a different world, have become an American, after getting involved in a relationship of unclear designation with an older German woman who managed a hotel where he worked maintaining elevators. But World War I scotched their future, not just on nationality grounds, with Frank feeling obliged as the product of a military family to go back and enlist.

He ended up in the Royal Flying Corps, initially as a ground-crew engineer, and at some point along the journey became close friends with another left-arm spinner, Colin Blythe of Kent, who trained Frank's bowling. In 1916, he got news of Blythe's death at Passchendaele, and that may have been what spurred Frank to start flying as a spotter for machine gunners.

Any flyer who survived was incredibly lucky, and Frank finished the war in England at Flowerdown airfield in Hampshire. That meant that by the time cricket resumed in 1919, Frank had qualified to play for the county. As we mentioned in another story, experienced players were thin on the ground that season, and it happened that Hampshire boss Lionel Tennyson knew of Frank through Blythe. Frank's dad had died before the war, so there was nobody to disappoint, and having already met and married his wife, Eva, Frank needed to make a living.

This is how, in July 1919 at the age of 30, Frank Ryan became a first-class cricketer. And the thing is, he was bloody good. He was tall, releasing his left-arm orthodox from a height that offered loop and drift. He had great accuracy and could turn the ball a long way. He had a decent first two seasons from limited opportunities, taking 63 wickets in a middling team. There were just two problems.

One was Frank Ryan, who loved to get tanked, have a bet, and chase women. The other was Lionel Tennyson, who loved to get tanked, have a bet, and chase women.

Lord Tennyson, as the title styled him, toff grandson of the poet, had a lot more money to lose, whereas Frank's gambling always had him broke. Perhaps there were differences over bets paid, perhaps over one's comments on the other's social life. Frank was a professional, while rich amateurs typically assumed themselves to be socially superior. However it happened, rather than bonding over shared interests, these two judged the other's foibles from the shaky foundations of their own.

Frank's other weakness on the drink, besides blowing his cash, was blowing his top. That hot temper would be lifelong. So, halfway through the 1920 season, after a trip to Liverpool in July, he walked out on the club. And we do mean *walked*. Needing a job but short of a train fare, he went on foot to Bristol to see if he could rekindle that old flame at Gloucestershire via a Flying Corps colleague. When that didn't pan out he was recommended to try Glamorgan, with the Welsh county soon to gain first-class status. He kept on walking to Swansea.

Showing up ragged and dishevelled in the pouring rain, wandering into the clubhouse, Frank looked like an itinerant because he was one. Club officials were mystified when he asked to have a net. But they let him have one, and remarkably on that evidence everybody struck a deal. First, he had to qualify for Glamorgan, which meant living in Cardiff for two years. His first championship match for the county came in 1923, when he was 34.

But that's when he flourished. In his first full season for Glamorgan, Frank took 106 wickets at 22. His second, 126 at 14. His third and best season, 139 wickets at 17, included the number at the top of this chapter, 8 for 41 against Derbyshire. That came after 5 for 19 in the first innings, one of the four times that season that he took 10 in a match.

He'd also qualified to play for Wales in an era when they aspired to be a Test team too, turning out against Scotland, Ireland, and the West Indies. He set up a win against the Scots with the bat, making his career-best score of 52 not out, and a win over West Indies with eight wickets, a huge moment for Welsh cricket. In his two Windies matches he knocked over the great Learie Constantine four times.

In those three seasons the drinking had eased a bit, but by 1926 he was back into it. That also meant he was back into fights with club officials and a rotating roster of captains, along with anybody else who might get in the way. This era produced the two most infamous Ryan travel stories – and it was away from home where he seemed to do his worst work.

In one, he was so wasted that he forgot where the team's lodgings were, so he slept under the covers at the cricket ground to await the next day. In the second, on the lash after a Lancashire game but with a game at home the next day, he decided he was having too good a time to join the rest of the team on their train, and much later took a taxi the 200-odd miles from Manchester to Swansea. Dropping the stonking bill on the Glamorgan secretary's desk, it's probably apocryphal that he called triumphantly, 'Ryan never lets you down!' But it fits the vibe.

Often, though, he could still do the job on the field. Ending the 1927 season, Arthur Carr's Nottinghamshire were an imposing side poised to secure the title, needing only a draw against a still weak Glamorgan. Frank took five wickets in the first innings to limit them to 233, then joined with Jack Mercer to sweep them a second time for 61, an innings victory that denied Nottinghamshire the championship.

In 1930, when Maurice Turnbull took over the team, Frank had a captain he liked. He returned to top form, 134 wickets including another eight-for. In August he got a crack against the touring Australians and showed his class: six wickets in the first innings, including the US tourists Bradman, McCabe, and

Vic Richardson. If his teammates had remembered how to bat, Glamorgan would have given the Australians a shake.

If he was ever close to playing for England, 1930 was the year, but his age being north of 40 was less of an obstacle than his reputation as a pisshead. And by 1931, Glamorgan were sinking into financial ruin. By the end of August, Frank had cracked a landmark, sneaking up to 1013 career wickets at 21, but ahead of the next season the club desperately cut costs, including their professional players.

Soon to turn 43, Frank was done, drifting into league cricket for a few years before World War II broke out. Too old for action, he ended up in the intelligence service – remarkably, because he had learned to speak German during his likely love affair in New York all those years earlier. He was probably monitoring letters and broadcasts, but with his ability to socialise, he might have been great undercover. And though he died in 1954, in true Frank style the details are uncertain. Cricinfo says January 5th, *Wisden* January 6th, *The Cricketer* January 7th. Where was he born? When did he die? Where did he sleep last night? Who knows. He's Frank Ryan.

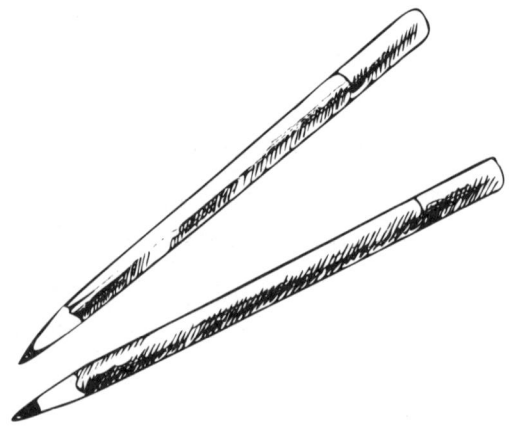

19

FATHER MARRIOTT IS NOT A PRIEST

11.96

Clue sent by:
Elia Andrews

WE'VE HAD A FEW THEMES IN THIS BOOK. ONE IS old-timey spin bowlers, another is players who flourished for a moment but never again. Father Marriott, first name Charles, was both, as a 1920s leg spinner who took 11 for 96 in his one and only Test match. He also could have represented Ireland, got gassed at the Somme in World War I, and was one of the worst first-class batters on record. Oh, and he wasn't a priest.

Charles Stowell Marriott was born near Manchester but raised in Ireland and went to Trinity College in Dublin before the war. Trinity does have a record of first-class matches, which is why the playwright Samuel Beckett is the only person with a Cricinfo page as well as a Nobel Prize, but none of those games were in the non-reverend's era. Having survived the war after being, sent to serve at home with shell shock in 1917, he was demobilised and back to university at Cambridge in 1920, where he became Father Marriott to young teammates given his unfathomably advanced age of 24.

But it's more fun to think of him swapping the dog collar for his whites, so let's keep doing that. He qualified by birth to play for Lancashire, turning out a few times in between

Cambridge games, and whoever he was playing for, he took bags. Six wickets here, seven there, eight somewhere else; he would flit into a side, hoover up stats, then disappear. At one point, deep into 1921, he took at least one wicket for 30 innings straight, which got him into the Ashes squad but not the XI.

Then he didn't play for three years, working as a teacher of languages at Dulwich College. But those years of residence qualified him to play for Kent. Lord Harris, of the 1879 Sydney Riot fame, was still kicking about, and he kept badgering Father Marriott to flick the wrist again. And Lord Harris tended to get his way. Second game back, 10 wickets against local rivals Hampshire. More single-innings bags, then 11 in a match against his old team Lancashire. He got on the South Africa tour in 1924/25, but as in his Ashes call-up, he carried the drinks.

On he went, in the style of an amateur with other commitments. Where professional players would have more than 30 starts in a season, Father M would rock up for 10 or 11, during school holidays or near the end of term. Each season he would play a handful of games in June or July, then a glut through August. For his entire Kent career, he never played in April, May, or September. It probably worked out great for him, arriving late in summer when drier pitches were receptive to spin. Kent were happy to accommodate, the county profiting to the tune of 463 wickets.

Lord Harris died in 1932, and Father Marriott played two more seasons at his former pace before starting to wind down.

The last of those full slates, 1933, saw him finally picked for a Test match, the third against the West Indies. It was August, of course, the month he called his own, on a deck at The Oval where spinners sometimes prospered. England regular Hedley Verity was injured. England made 312 after a shaky start, Father M predictably was last in and made a duck.

After a rest day, England took the new ball and Nobby Clark the first three West Indian wickets, but then it was time to check in to the Marriott. He extracted the middle order, including the original West Indies superstar George Headley, who he defeated like a true spinner with a stumping. Then back he came to clean up the tail, finishing with 5 for 37. As so often before, a bag for the Father. And as so often before, a second bag to follow, with a long spell to take 6 for 59 and bank an innings win. Those are still the eighth best figures on debut.

Father Marriott did get on the tour to India and Sri Lanka a few months later and went alright in the tour matches but again didn't get a Test. He played the 1934 Australians in England for MCC but got pantsed, as most bowlers did by the 1934 Australians – Bradman didn't get many, but Ponsford and McCabe sure did. Soon to turn 39, there wasn't much road left for Father Marriott. He played a few more first-class games until 1938 but never for England again.

So where does that leave us? With 11 wickets at 8.7, he is the only Test bowler whose career stats have wickets in double figures and an average in single figures. Scott Boland briefly had him covered, with 14 wickets at 8.64 after two matches. Players would be happy to trade a dip in their stats for more chances to play the game, but if that chance doesn't come, staying top of a list must be some consolation.

All up, Father Marriott took 711 first-class wickets, with a whistle-worthy average of just over 20. On the flipside, he made 574 runs at 4.4. On the distinguished list of players with more wickets than runs, CS Marriott sits right next to CS Martin (NZ), a celebration both of sporting ineptitude and the willingness to keep on trying.

Get this: in a career spanning 178 hits and 18 seasons, Charles Marriott had never once reached 20 – until his very last match for Kent in 1937. After conceding a big score, his team put him up as nightwatchman opener in what must have been a farewell lark. Next morning, either Sussex were feeling sporting or he had a swing and some good fortune. His score of 21 was the team's second best, and his wicket set off a mighty collapse. When they followed on, he was back where he should be, batting at 11, stumped for the 52nd and final duck of his career.

We talk a lot about unlucky cricketers when it comes to timing and selection – you can build whole teams of Australians in the 1990s who are talked of as hard done by. And you could make the case, on the figures, that Charles Marriott is the unluckiest bowler to play at the highest level. On the other hand, the Father got a long first-class career played entirely on his terms, never had to turn up in the gloves-and-beanie months of the early season, and got to do all that because he walked away intact from Ypres and the Somme. You don't get much luckier than that.

20

THE MANY NAWABS OF PATAUDI

9.81

**Clue sent by:
Peta Dowling**

Sometimes, an obsession with a cricketing figure can develop from superficial beginnings. In this case, it is simply very satisfying to say out loud 'the Nawab of Pataudi'. Try it for yourself. It's even more satisfying when you learn that the annals of Test cricket contain two Nawabs of Pataudi, so you get the chance to say it twice.

Once you get intrigued, more questions arise. What is a Nawab? Where is Pataudi? Why were there two of them? Why was one named Tiger? And were they actually any good at cricket?

To start at the end, the answer is yes, they were exceptional. In colonial India, Pataudi was one of many small 'princely states' with local monarchs. This particular one was near Delhi and has since been absorbed into the state of Haryana. The Nawab was the prince of the princely state, and Iftikhar Ali Khan Pataudi inherited that title in 1917, at the age of seven. In pre-partition India, the family was from the Muslim north, with roots tracing back to Afghanistan.

Being a Nawab, naturally he went to a fancy school in Lahore and got personal batting training before going to study at Oxford. He helped beat a couple of MCC sides in single-day matches for an Indian side in 1926 but didn't get a shot in Oxford's first-class team for two years, then was deep into a second unimpressive season before something clicked. Under the pump in the grudge match against Cambridge (captained by Frank Ryan's favourite skipper, Maurice Turnbull), the Nawab pulled out 106 in the first innings and 84 in the second, top-scoring both times to save the game.

That was 1929. He made three more tons in 1930, then how about this first-class sequence in 1931: start with 169 against Gloucestershire, 4 and 52 against a jazz-hat team, 42 against the touring Kiwis, 35 and 183 not out against an Army XI, 165 and 100 against Surrey, 138 and 68 against another exhibition side, topped off with 238 not out against his old mates at Cambridge. The Oxford–Cambridge record had been set the previous day with Cambridge's opener making 201, but the prince said not to worry, he would top it. Next day, that's what he did. His record lasted 70 years.

No surprise then that he got a call-up for the Gents versus Players match, then the tour to Australia in 1932/33. He didn't mind the bounce in Perth: consecutive tons against Western Australia and a pretty strong Australian XI in a warm-up. Our pal Laurie Nash bowled him in another tour match, but a few games later the Nawab was walking onto the SCG on Test debut and made a century there as well. Another followed next innings against Tasmania. An Indian royal was dominating for England.

But that didn't help when he attracted the ire of his captain, Douglas Jardine. Bradman missed that first Test, which England won easily, but returned for Melbourne. Jardine intensified his bodyline tactics: short at the ribs or head with a ring of leg-side catchers waiting for a fended chance. After seeing enough of this to decide that he didn't like it, the Nawab refused to move into one of those positions, while Jardine derided him as 'a conscientious objector' – that's not really an insult, Doug.

So after missing out with the bat in Melbourne, he was dropped. Imagine that. A Test century in the previous outing, four tons in nine first-class hits on tour, 601 runs at 66, and gone because he wasn't vicious enough. A quote often attributed to him on tour about Jardine was, 'I am told he has his good points. In three months I have yet to see them.'

Now playing for Worcestershire in county cricket, he made a spate of double hundreds in 1933 and 1934, then a big unbeaten hundred for an England side in a Test warm-up against a trial team called The Rest: once again deflating rival skipper Maurice Turnbull. That got the Nawab into the first Test during the famous 1934 Ashes, but that Australian side was unstoppable, and he didn't keep his spot. It was his third and last Test for England.

But Test cricket in India was now bubbling away, and there was a movement to get the Nawab captaining a side. Restrictions on players moving between national teams didn't exist then, and it seemed intuitive that he could lead India just as well as play for England. He was strangely reticent. For India's first Test in 1932, which was in England, he was being suggested as leader but withdrew. He didn't travel with Jardine to India in 1934, and when India next came to England in 1936, he was initially supposed to captain but pulled out citing ill health.

It was after World War II when he finally turned out for India in a Test, leading the side on a tour of England in 1946. He had a decent average of 47 across the tour, making our Story Time number of 981 runs as they beat four of the county sides, and naturally he tonned up once more in defeating Cambridge. But he struggled in the Tests and ended his international career there – the only player to have appeared for England and India, with three Tests apiece.

Not that he believed he was done with cricket: he was 36 when that tour ended and 41 when he declared that he was planning a return to Worcestershire – but he never got back to England. In true princely fashion, he died that year from a heart attack while playing polo. It was a rough present for his son, Mansur Ali Khan Pataudi, who became the new Nawab on his 11th birthday.

Young Tiger Pataudi, though, would make a lifetime's habit of getting on with things. Within five years he was playing first-class cricket, and he would go on to a far greater Test career than his father: India's youngest captain, skippering 40 matches out of 46, six hundreds – and all of it done with the use of one eye.

His nickname probably came from childhood, but the origin story was retrofitted to cite the way he prowled the covers. Stylish and athletic, batting with flair, he was a player who made an impression. Mike Brearley wrote, 'On the field he had presence, a regal touch; one's eyes would be drawn to him, as eyes have been drawn to Imran Khan, Viv Richards, Ian Botham. A proper arrogance, or as Bishan Bedi put it, an imperious charm.'

Packed off young to an English boarding school, he may have taken some satisfaction in his 1068 runs for Winchester, breaking the school record set by his late father's least beloved England teammate, Douglas Jardine.

By then Tiger had already debuted in top-flight cricket for Sussex, aged 16, and while his early seasons produced sporadic appearances and no big scores, he did better for Oxford. After three tons in his first season and being named captain of the university to start his second, he got on a hot streak early in 1961: three consecutive hundreds plus a 79, totalling 432 runs for two dismissals, then another run of six consecutive 50-plus scores ending with 108.

Two weeks later, he and wicketkeeper Robin Waters were playing for Oxford away against Sussex – their own county – when Waters drove them back to the team hotel. An oncoming car cut a corner and smashed into theirs. Teammates found them bleeding at the scene. The scorecard shows Waters, who had been not out overnight, retired hurt for 0, and Tiger absent hurt. Glass from the windscreen had pierced Tiger's eyes, and only one was saved.

Waters was also hurt, and while he recovered to play on, a promising career delivered much less than it might have. Cricketer-journalist Robin Marlar said that he carried 'deep mental scars'. Having moved to Dublin, Waters later recounted that years on, when the Indian team visited Ireland, Tiger invited him to dinner. 'He urged me to forget about the mishap. He would say it was in his destiny to lose the eye.'

Destiny or not, it was Tiger's own stubbornness that kept him going. The accident was on July 1st, yet astonishingly, he played his next first-class match on October 31st, making a half-century and taking a wicket in a Ranji Trophy game. By December, he was making his Test debut for India against England. It was an extraordinary feat of will to get back in the nets only weeks after surgery, training his brain to adjust after initially seeing double. His luck, such as it was, was that his right eye took the damage, and as a right-hander, his leading eye was his left. Squinting his right eye, shaded behind a cap brim pulled low, he found a way to track the ball.

Tiger always said that his batting never reached what it could have been after the accident, but it worked well enough to make 64 in his second Test and 103 in his third, while India won the series. By their next, Tiger was captain at 21 years old, yet to graduate university. His team went down to Frank Worrell's West Indies, but this was an era when Indian sides were often heavily outmatched. Nevertheless, Tiger found a way to have his teams compete hard, especially at home

They fought England to a standstill across five Tests, Tiger with his career-best 203 not out. They drew 1–1 while beating Australia in a match for the first time, a thriller by two wickets in which both innings were built around Tiger's 86 and 53. They beat New Zealand at home in 1965, with a couple of Tiger hundreds, then away in 1968 for India's first overseas series win, with his runs again influential. Nine wins and a dozen draws from his 40 matches in charge show a side punching above its weight. More important than results, Tiger gave an example of resilience.

As did his coda: having ceded captaincy to Ajit Wadekar after 1969, Tiger answered the call when Wadekar abruptly retired, coming back in 1974 to lead one more series. To that point, India had beaten the West Indies in one Test out of 28, and it became one out of 30 after Tiger dislocated his finger in the first match and missed the second, with the team demoralised and smashed in his absence. Yet somehow he turned his players around to win the next two, forcing the West Indies to lift for a fifth-Test decider. Gundappa Viswanath's batting can take much of the credit, but some has to go to the man in charge of the dressing room.

Tiger would be the last Nawab, with princely titles abolished under constitutional reform in 1971. His children and grandchildren switched to that other modern stream of royalty, Bollywood acting. But from 2007 to 2025, Indian Test tours of England were played for the Pataudi Trophy, named after the dual national Nawab Sr. The Nawab Jr lived to see his father honoured in this way, and died before the trophy was controversially superseded by one boringly named after modern players. On Tiger's death in 2011, his will directed that his one working eye should be donated for a transplant. Whoever ended up with it got a good one.

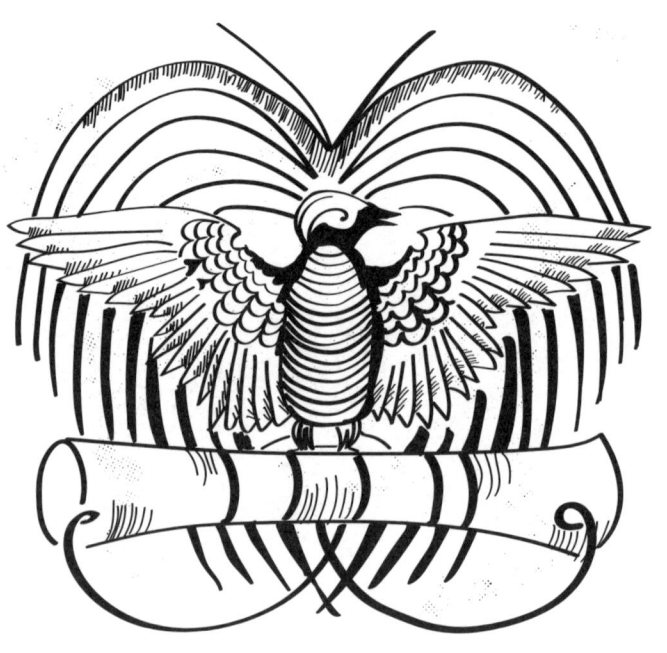

21

THE MIGHTY WINDIES TOUR OF PAPUA NEW GUINEA

10.70

Clue sent by:
Rafael Szumer

WHEN YOU THINK ABOUT THE MIGHTY WEST Indies of cricketing lore, the fast-bowling machine with the batting swagger, their time really begins in 1975 after winning the first World Cup that English summer. So which countries do you most readily think of them taking down? Australia, with pace weapons in reply? England, to settle a historical grudge? India, who they built a great rivalry with? You'd get a long way down the list of nations before coming to Papua New Guinea.

But look closer, and it's not as unlikely as it might seem. Papua New Guinea was the newest entrant to the list of nations in September 1975, just after that first World Cup. Independence had been a long time coming: Australian forces had occupied PNG since 1914, after kicking out German colonists during World War I and later turning back the invading Japanese in World War II. Self-government eventually arrived through a peaceful process driven by the two countries' respective leaders Gough Whitlam and Michael Somare.

In the same era, Caribbean countries were discarding British rule. The West Indies still existed as a cricket team but less so as a political confederation, as Jamaica, Trinidad and

The Mighty Windies Tour of Papua New Guinea

Tobago, Barbados, Guyana, and Grenada all went their own way by 1974. That meant that in September 1975, you had an affinity between newly independent island nations from the Caribbean to the Coral Sea. Heading to a Test series in Australia, the Windies players were happy to visit on the way; as tour manager Esmond Kentish said, 'to give the people of Papua an idea of what we are doing on our side of the world'.

As it turned out, October 1975 was an extraordinary time to be padding up in the region. With East Timor also about to declare independence, this time in an armed struggle with Portugal, Indonesia was preparing to invade as the new colonial power. One week before our first cricket match, Indonesian special forces murdered the Balibo Five: a group of Australian TV journalists reporting on military incursions into Timor that Indonesia was denying existed. The full invasion would follow in December.

Meanwhile, the cricketers were heading up to Lae and a pitch of canvas on concrete at the University Ground. Spectators were seated on the grass, and there was a rudimentary boundary-side public address system on a card table. But if all this reflected a social series, it was a serious West Indies team that rocked up. Roy Fredericks, Gordon Greenidge, Alvin Kallicharran, Clive Lloyd, Viv Richards, Deryck Murray, Keith Boyce, Bernard Julien, and Andy Roberts were all there. The only World Cup finalists missing were Rohan Kanhai and Vanburn Holder, replaced by young gun Lawrence Rowe and champion spinner Lance Gibbs.

Some incredible video survives, not match footage

but fragments shot wandering the perimeter, including a young Viv sweating bullets in the humidity. There's a strong Australian flavour to proceedings, like the heavily accented voice on the loudspeaker getting names wrong, or saying, 'I think all the spectators should join together to give the two teams the old Aussie hip hip hooray.' Richie Benaud was there, having met Clive Lloyd at Port Moresby airport, Clive rocking a full safari suit, Richie in an incredibly 70s floral shirt that looked like he was wearing a couch. And there were plenty of Australian expat players: PNG had received ICC associate status in 1973, but that didn't mean much by 1975.

There were four or five Papuan players in the first match in Lae, the team styled as a PNG Combined XI, and six in the second match in Port Moresby, where they were playing more simply as Papua New Guinea. And they gave it a tilt. Lae was a 25-over match, and the home team only lost three wickets making 107 – there's the number from our clue. There's confusion on the scorecard with West Indies making 177, because after running down the real target they wanted to keep giving the crowd a show. But with West Indies losing eight wickets, six PNG bowlers had something to brag about.

Amini Park in Moresby the next day had more facilities, with indoor radio booths for commentators in English and Pidgin. This match was 40 overs, and when PNG crashed to 5 for 33, Lloyd helped by swapping his fast bowlers for part-time spin, the home side recovering to 115.

If the chase was supposed to be easy, it wasn't quite. Greenidge had made a duck in the first match and was out for 3 here. Rowe made 11, Murray 1, and Kallicharran 6. It was 4 for 53 when the captain stepped in to settle things with Fredericks, but the opener fell for 35 and Viv followed for 4. A feller named Charles Harrison had three of the six to fall, the score was 97, and the West Indies still needed 19 to win. Could PNG dare to dream?

In a word, no. Lloyd stayed, and Bernard Julien stuck with him. But even that moment of possibility existing was unlikely. On reaching the target, the Windies again carried on batting to entertain the crowd, reaching 201. But they lasted 31 overs out of 41, so PNG were able to claim the distinct honour of having bowled the West Indies out.

The achievement was celebrated with good cheer at a welcome dinner that night hosted by Governor-General John Guise. He had been a star junior cricketer himself, and he pretended to be reluctant to share his tale of making a club triple century as a young man. Benaud chatted in the crowd. Trays circulated with snacks straight out of the 1970s *Women's Weekly Cookbook*. Windies manager Kentish charmed the crowd: 'I would like to thank you for the very warm welcome that you have given us, not only in words but in temperature.'

In time, the PNG cricket team became the Barramundis and won their first two official ODI matches in 2014. That was almost 40 years on from Clive Lloyd at Lae. Almost 50 years later, in Guyana, they nearly beat the West Indies in a T20 World Cup. There was nothing lighthearted or social about that match, which turned on a missed review and one big over at the death. In time, perhaps Papua New Guinea's cricketing star will further rise, decades on from the time when they first took on the best.

22

THE GREATEST TEST INNINGS OF ALL?

2.70

Clue sent by:
Christopher Weinberg & Matt Gaynor

Arguing about the greatest innings ever is like cricket itself: utterly pointless, irresistible to lunatics, and highly enjoyable if you're into things that are likely to drag on for days. You can endlessly dissect the variables: pitch, weather, quirks of grounds, strength of bowling, difficulty of the team's situation on the field or the player's situation off it.

We can't resist jokes about Don Bradman; it's the only option when he was treated as sacred for so long. But even being facetious, and even when his stories are so familiar, there are still times when you stop to consider what one or other of his numbers *actually* means, and the answer still whacks you upside the head. Using the criteria above, it's hard to argue with *Wisden's judges* when they decided that Bradman's 270 was the greatest knock of the 20th century. Melbourne 1937 wasn't his biggest score, but it was his best.

For a start, consider the concept of a five-Test series. Shortly after this book comes out, the 160th of these will be played. Of those, six have had the teams locked at 2–2 going into the fifth. Five of those six started with a team losing twice, fighting back to level the score, then running out of steam and

The Greatest Test Innings of All?

losing the decider. Only once did a team trail by two, then come back to win three in a row. That turnaround hinged on two things: Bradman's captaincy and Bradman's score.

It was the Australian summer of 1936/37, meaning it was the first English visit since Bodyline, and you'd better believe that Australians were still pissed. Partly they were mad at the tactics, mostly they were mad that the tactics had worked. Australia replied with carnage in England in 1934, but that wasn't revenge enough: the Aussie crowd was ginned up on home soil. Bradman was already the best batter in history, plus he was captain, so he led the team out … to be utterly destroyed in Brisbane, then in Sydney.

They were all out for 58 in one Test, out for 80 in the next, while Bradman's batting included a duck from his first ball and a duck from his second. By New Year's Day of 1937, they faced humiliation in straight sets. And it didn't get much better on the first day with 6 for 181. On day two, overnight rain carried on until after lunch, so they resumed on a wet pitch and lost three more quickly.

It was 9 for 200, nowhere near enough, but with wicketkeeper Bert Oldfield still there, the normal course would be to hope that the last man in could help him scrape a few more runs. Except, instead of looking up at the scoreboard, Bradman looked down at the mucky pitch. And in a move that in itself is pretty bloody bolshie, he decided that batting first in a timeless Test was still a good moment to declare.

England in response started alright, though scatters of rain continued. And then, in no time at all, they got ripped apart:

one moment 2 for 56, the next losing 7 for 20. The ball was doing all sorts: erratic bounce, impossible to time. Having bowled fewer than 30 overs, Bradman realised his bowlers were taking wickets too quickly. If his team had to bat again on that mess before the day was out, they might lose a similar pile, which would let England chase on subsequent days as the pitch improved.

To slow his roll, he started pushing catchers back, creating gaps, dragging out the innings. England got wise to this, and after agonising about the right course, declared at 9 for 76. With 40 minutes left to bat, and plenty of risk inherent, Bradman went even more sensational. He flipped the goddamn batting order.

The team had three tail-end wrist spinners: Chuck Fleetwood-Smith, Bill O'Reilly, and Frank Ward. Chuck, the number 11 who Bradman had declared on rather than giving him a hit first time around, got promoted to open the batting. Bill, the original number nine, got sent up alongside him, the pair walking onto the MCG at the top of the order.

The rationale was that their wickets were less important, and every ball they faced was one less that day for the specialist bats. It might have looked mad when O'Reilly chipped his first ball back to the bowler, and madder still when Frank Ward, the original number 10, was sent in next. But it worked. Helped by a reprieve for bad light, the two spinners made it to stumps.

That was Saturday, and Sunday was a rest day. By Monday, the pitch was improving, getting better each hour. Knowing that he was the key wicket, Bradman held himself back. Keith

Rigg was the only player to bat in the same position in both innings, keeping his spot at four. At five and six came the usual openers, Bill Brown and Jack Fingleton, to keep blocking away. And finally, at seven, Bradman.

When the captain walked in at 5 for 97, this was the scene. Australia were 221 ahead, but England would get to chase on an improving pitch with as much time as they wanted. Australia still needed big runs, and failure to get them meant losing the series. They had batting in reserve, in Stan McCabe and Len Darling, but rejigged orders often don't work out.

The bowling was quality. Hedley Verity, left-arm spinner, was as close as Bradman had to a nemesis, and had knocked him over for 13 first dig. Bill Voce was half of the Bodyline pair, gobbling up wickets on his own, and Gubby Allen was a quality seamer. Leg spinners occasionally gave Bradman trouble, and England had two, in Walter Robins and Jim Sims.

Public interest was at an all-time high: there were nearly 90,000 in on this third day, and the full match held the Test record of over 350,000 until the Boxing Day Test of 2024. There was the pressure of all those eyes watching and the newspapers poised, with Bradman's captaincy riding on the result. On a personal level, throw in that he was now crook with the flu after those wet days on the field and that, a couple of months earlier, both he and McCabe had lost newborn babies.

It's a hell of a roll call of factors. In that context, with all that to think about, Bradman dug in to see out the day with 56 not out. On day four, he batted on, and on, through the entire day. When England set the field back, wanting to tire out a sick player by making him run, he kept on running.

Some newspapers reported the patience of an innings 'in which he subordinated his natural desires to the determination to place Australia in an unassailable position.' Others emphasised his opening up later in the day as 'a mixture of safety and daring. His daring in stealing runs was remarkable and he drove, hooked, and pulled with great freedom'. His old teammate Arthur Mailey was effusive: 'some of his cuts and hooks and pulls today made one marvel ... Those of the tired fieldsmen to whom I spoke after the match agreed that Bradman was the master batsman, the inventor of new and daring shots, the creator of a new technique.'

Fingleton stuck with him most of the day, making his own century. In a photograph from a drinks break, the two are flat on their backs on the grass. By the time Fingleton edged behind for 136, they had added 346, and the only two bigger partnerships in Tests were also Bradman jobs. But he wasn't done, cracking 38 of the first 50 runs in a stand with McCabe, reaching the day's end on 248 not out. The next day he made 22 more, hitting out at nine down. Australia were all out for 564, England were set 689, and there was all the time in the world to chisel out the win.

Bradman batted close to eight hours for what is still the highest score from number seven. He batted a bit over seven hours in the next Test for another second-innings double ton, this time worth 212. And in the decider, back in Melbourne, he top-scored again with 169 to lead his team to an innings win, three on the bounce, and a series pulled from the fire. It's outrageous, and it hinges on 270 at number seven. In a career full of bonkers performances, even Bradman couldn't top this one. And if Bradman couldn't top it, you'd better believe nobody else can either.

ACKNOWLEDGEMENTS

Historical research has many forebears, and our collation of it has led to sources too diffuse to catalogue. Buy cricket books – the world is full of good ones. Our particular acknowledgement goes to the historical research of Andrew Hignell, Bernard Whimpress, Abhishek Mukerjee, Arunabha Sengupta, Giles Lowcock, David Frith, Simon Wilde, and Gideon Haigh; the great statisticians Andrew Samson, Ric Finlay, and Andy Zaltzman; our Nerd Pledge sleuth crew Pat Rodgers, Matt May, Sean McGivern, Glenn Finkelde, and Thomas Melia; and regular co-hosts Daniel Norcross and Bharat Sundaresan. Also thanks to the contributors to 160 years of the *Wisden Cricketers' Almanack*, to everyone who has worked on the Trove newspaper archive at the National Library of Australia, and especially to all of you who have sent in a pledge and set us after another story.

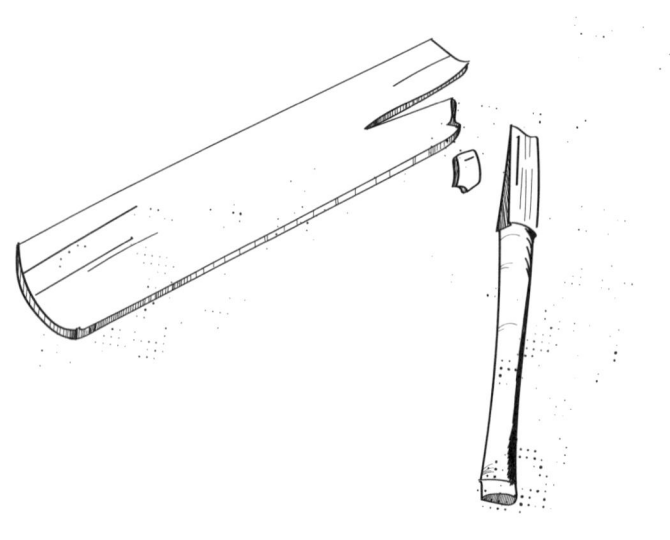